Inspired by Rosa Parks's Courage and Sitting on the Bus: (v.4)
How to Find Inspiration For Our Difficult Times

Rosa Parks's Poetry of Courage and Redemption
US Blossoms and Harvest Delights Series

In appreciation of
California's Multi-ethnic Groups, Cultures, Wine,
Fruits, Beaches and Landscape

To the diversity and beauty of the United States of America!

Multicultural Writer and Author: Joseph J. Charles

http://poetrybusinessblog.blogspot.com
And

http://bestsellerpicks.blogspot.com

ISBN:
978-1-257-08365-7

Dedication and Thanks

This book would not be possible without the dedication and hard labor of our farmers, growers and the various organizations that advocate on behalf of California agriculture. I want to give thanks for all the juicy and beautiful fruits we have come to expect every year. The Central Valley of California is the "fruit basket" of the world.

This book is a tribute to the stewardship and sustainability spirit that most Californians possess. I have learned that to better appreciate California one has to be an outdoors person. Think about the sun, sand, sea, mountains and snowfields, dunes, orchards, wildlife and the vast expanse of farmland that the Golden State proudly and generously offers to the tourist. How about Highway 99? Who can forget all the little towns that you meet along the way? You can decide to go to Yosemite, Kings Canyon or Napa Valley, Santa Barbara, San Diego or Pismo Beach.

This book is dedicated to everybody who loves California, eats the fruits of the Central Valley, enjoys her famous recreation sites such as Yosemite, Hollywood, Santa Monica, LA area, Squaw Valley, Santa Barbara and many more.

I thank all my readers who, after reading "The Long Lost Garden of Eden" have told me about their interest in my second book. So here it is.

This book is dedicated to Caleb, Cassandra and Colby. Caleb, this is your book!

Thanks for allowing me to give you my interpretation of what it is like to live in California.

Thanks to Florence and Felicia Paredes, Arthur Okumoto, Gudo Hallstone, Sonja Sher, Ramona Noriega and countless others for their support.

Finally, this book is dedicated to the diversity of the United States of American that makes this country stronger!

Table of Contents

1. Dedication and Thanks
2. Temporary Problems, Eternal Glory
3. Bridges of California
4. Pastoral Delights
5. Gold Nuggets
6. The Walls of Jerusalem, The Walls of Fresno
7. Hypergraphia
8. This Land Is Our Land
9. Such Delights Of The Granadas
10. Pho Soup Fusion
11. All of a Sudden, Rapture
12. Abrahamic Promise
13. Autumn's Bare Limbs
14. Sticks in the Land
15. Wine and Worms
16. Influx of Cheap Labor
17. Freeway and Highway Crosses
18. Decadence
19. Superb Bowl or Super Bowl Hyperbole
20. Every Inch and Each Act
21. Island Figs
22. Firefighters and the Big One
23. Cry Over Manzanar
24. Open-field Nuts Check
25. Half-life of Parents
26. Harvest Display
27. Harvesting Delights of the Garden
28. Odes to Kings River
29. Liquid Gold, Sierra Snowpack
30. Lite Lit Bites
31. Lost Meditations
32. Open Range, More Steak Please
33. Peach and Nectarine Bites
34. The Good Life. Go Nuts! Will You?
35. Poetry Like Water
36. Roosting Marvels, Roosting Headache
37. Spirit Fog
38. Tamales For The Holidays
39. The Redeemer and the Redeemed
40. Head to Big Sur For Romance and Meditation
41. College Reality on Alcohol Abuse
42. Farming Waste Comes With The Territory

43. California Outdoors Cooking
44. Summer Grilling in California
45. Teach Your Kids The Right Way
46. Obsession and Addiction to Cleaning
47. Fresno's Hip Spots
48. Los Angeles and Jay Leno's Cars
49. What's Special About California's Multiethnic, Multifaith….
50. The Museum of Tolerance
51. Pismo Beach, California Central Coast
52. Sacramento, The State Capital of California
53. San Francisco, The City By The Bay
54. Santa Monica, The Liveliest City on Highway 1
55. The Unfinished Business, The Vacuum Job
56. A Living Testament To Our Heroes
57. The American Good Life
58. The Migration To The North
59. Clovis, California
60. A Brand New Day In San Francisco
61. Water and the Blossom
62. Blooming Orchards
63. Harvest Ladder
64. Golden Vineyards
65. Sanger, CA
66. The Vast Wilderness
67. Convivialis: Food and Romance
68. Chili on top of Hot Dogs
69. Fallen Angels
70. Prophecy and Revelations

Copyright 01-17-2011 Joseph Jony Charles

http://bestsellerpicks.blogspot.com
No parts of this book can be copied or reproduced without the written authorization of its author.

Mr. Charles is the author of the well-acclaimed "The Long Lost Garden of Eden," a tribute to the farmers, growers, farmworkers and consumers of California-grown fruits. It's available at http://shopnowshop.tripod.com, http://bookstore.shopnowshop.com, amazon.com, Barnes and Noble, Borders and many other booksellers.

Once more, Central Valley residents, thanks for your support and encouragement!

Happy Reading!

Rosa Sat Down

Rosa sat so
Martin Luther could walk
[She was tired of giving in for far too long]
Martin walked so Obama could run
[Martin walked and marched with his followers. He was a true leader]
 [Without the works of those leaders laboring even during slavery, 1950s, 1960s, Obama would not be able to be where he is at right now]
Obama ran....so our
Children could fly
[Without the sacrifices of Medgar Evers,Emmet Till, Martin Luther King and countless others, the greatest chapter of world history and transfer of power would not be written]

So it is up to us to keep the flames of freedom and liberty going
By investing in our kids, the future of this great nation!

Rosa Parks Sat on the Bus After a Long Journey

Martin Luther King was a student of Henry David Thoreau
who protested slavery and other unjust laws
Nobody thought that the Morehouse College student
would become a civil rights leader
Nobody thought much about Rosa Parks either
A seamstress who rode the public bus to and from her job
at a local department store
Martin L. King embraced non-violence championed by Mahatma Gandhi
Rosa has long been a member of her local chapter of NAACP
Rosa refused to give up her seat. She was tired of giving in
She stared down the bus driver and the other passengers
All of them wanted her out of the prime seat. None of them was defending her
Change was about to come in the 1950s and 1960s.
Who would have thought that this single act would be

the start of the modern civil rights movement?
Everyone counts. Rosa sat so we can stand up together

Rosa Parks's Montgomery Ride, Poetic History
by JJC, Feb. 2009

Tired and hungry, Rosa only cared about catching a ride
Her job at the department store meant the world to her
But she quietly cared about how her black brothers and sisters were being treated by the government and the Montgomery bus officials
After a long day and after witnessing all the hard news, she wanted to sit down
Rosa got on the bus in Montgomery, Alabama. Instead of going to the back of the bus
She sat down in a front seat. All hells broke loose!
Dogs could be unleashed on her tired and frail body. She could be flushed out of the seat
with powerful water hoses besides all the stares from fellow passengers
"'Who does she think she is to brave the front seat of the bus'"
The bus driver got into her face and asked her to move.
But Rosa parks refused. The news about Rosa Parks's arrest traveled quickly
among the Black residents of Montgomery and the Black leaders had to have a plan

The event of December 1, 1955 led to the December 5, 1955 Montgomery Bus boyccott. Montgomery city officials would soon realize that if the Blacks walked to work and school instead of riding the public bus, the city would lose money.

Black and White civil rights leaders gave as many rides as they could in their own private cars. But the majority of passengers walked many miles for many weeks.

"If Black people could not sit wherever they wanted, then they would refuse to take the buses."

That peaceful protest was very successful. Driving While Black, Martin L. King was arrested by local police who said he was speeding.

Car pools were organized by black as well as white leaders. The boycott lasted over a year.

Finally, the Supreme Court of the United States proclaimed that laws separating whites and blacks on the Montgomery buses had to end.

The Women of NAACP: Myrlie Evers-Williams and Rosa Parks
By Joseph J. Charles

Myrlie Evers-Williams became a young widow

who had three children to raise by herself

She heeded her late husband's last word, "take care of my children."

The assassination of Medgar Evers, a WWII veteran who wanted to see change

had a lasting impact on the Evers children, Myrlie and the rest of the country

Medgar became a sacrificial lamb, the strong and intelligent NAACP field director

Myrlie was not ready to forget the seeds her husband had planted
"Evers fought segregation of schools and public places, struggled to increase black voter registration, led business boycotts, brought attention to the murders and lynchings of Blacks, like the slaying of black teenager Emmett Till, planned protest to allow negroes access to Mississippi's public beaches...."

Myrlie raised her children and continued to work for the advancement of colored people
She became the chairperson of NAACP from 1995 to 1998.

She kept her promise to her husband, Medgar Evers who wanted to see change in Jackson, Mississippi.

Through the work of many others and after many years, change has gradually come to America

""I am just so thankful that I have lived long enough -- and have been able to participate in -- this change," said Myrlie Evers-Williams.

Medgar Evers and Martin L. King had laid down their lives for the movement so change could occur

During all these years, Myrlie has witnessed and kept the flames of freedom going.

Bridges Of California

"To live, men need bread as well as beauty,
Oxygen as well as meditation."

Why should we fear life's restless stream?
Why should we postpone our dream?
Why should we lose faith in the face of terror,
Calamity, weapons of mass destruction, horror,
germs, biological threats and a torrid storm?
We must continue to search for answers with fervor
Don't we still have the Golden Gate bridge?
On her wide decks, reflect on her awesome form and history
Don't we still have the peaks of the Sierra Nevada?
Don't we still have the Hoover Dam
Where water gets corralled to quench many a ram?
Don't we still have the striking beauty of Yosemite,
Kings Canyon, Big Sur, the coastal range, and Sequoia Park?
As resplendent as they can be in the sizzling Summer sun,
the bridges of California still loom mountain high, full of fun
Don't their strong piers still grip the ocean floor?
San Francisco-Oakland Bay bridge, Golden Gate bridge,
Richmond-San Rafael bridge, San Mateo-Hayward bridge
We appreciate thy steel arms which support and facilitate
commerce, transportation and quality time
They connect people with people as they link shore with shore
O bridges of California, massive monuments to men's
Technological advances, determination, and great vision
be exalted on high and break the enveloping foggy mist
Jewels of the west, may your high lights continue to shine
From all the world, tourists will ride through your gates
With pride, your towers will continue to pierce the sky

Pastoral Delights

Numerous heads of cattle are grazing on the grassland
under a spring-like weather in the middle of Winter
Not far from a lone oak tree, the steers concentrate
on the tall non-native grass that grows in the sudden pools
A recent wind has cleared the ozone and the smog that tend
to block the view of the snow-capped Sierra Nevada mountains
From their hives on the edge of the fields,
the working bees of the central Valley have already realized
the appropriate weather conditions to fly from nectar to nectar
Most of them will return the next day to pollinate almond trees
There are no nuts without bees. Neither are there crops
without snow and water flowing down from the mountains

On such pre-spring days, who wants to think about ozone?
Yet, we know that this invisible gas is as sure as Spring,
Fall, and Summer. May this perfect picture last one more day!
The sun shines enough to break the cold and warm one's heart
in the backroads of Madera and Fresno counties.
Who wants to think about particulate matter or PM?
These solid materials get suspended in the air
of the San Joaquin Valley. We throw ourselves into many
outdoors activities. We breathe the soot, ash, diesel exhaust,
dust and nitrogen-containing chemicals
that rich and poor residents swim through. We are all equal
before air pollution. So are we with asthma attacks, heart attacks,
lung cancer, chest pain, wheezing and many other weather-related ills.
Who wants to think about the days when kids can't play outside?
Who wants to think about the times
when football practices must be cancelled?
Bad air saps the energy of most valley residents

Isn't it time that we protect our heart?
Let everyday be Valentine's day
Loved ones will pay more attention
to their sweetheart's health.
Isn't it time we pay attention
to the air quality index?
We, Californians, enjoy outdoor activities
Yet, when the reading of the AQI is above 150,
we should heed forecasters' advice.
"Limit your outdoor activities. You should be concerned."
Soon the seasonal rainwater pools of Madera will be the sites
of beautiful wild flowers which will attract nature lovers

Let the ranchers join hands with the environmentalists
to preserve and fight off creeping encroachment,
hungry urban development and sprawls
The majestic rolls of the landscape are potent magnets
that will prevent future generations from enjoying
the unspoiled view and access to the Sierra Nevada range

Gold Nuggets

Organic peaches, nectarines, avocados, hay,
grapes, free-range cattle and chickens are
the new gold nuggets of Calif. farming
A new gold rush is on. It's time to convert
and change traditional growing practices
It's time to transition the fields
For three years, the farmer should not use
manufactured fertilizers and pesticides
It's a return to the land as the repository of many
systems of living organisms needing our stewardship
for preservation and continued production
Like gold mining, organic farming requires lots of work
The virtues of beneficial cover crops must be rediscovered
Weeds become the unconquered forts of the land
Gophers like to hide underneath these weeds
To cause major headaches to organic farmers
Weed control, gopher traps, ladybug and timely pruning
are their only weapons. A new focus on holistic health is born
The organic farmer is in a perpetual war against pests
to meet consumers' needs to have reliable agricultural products
Farmers, growers, ranchers and food processors are now giving
consumers what they want. We are willing to pay for it too!
Organic farming is a return to uncomplicated and natural principles
The consumers' perception of what's healthy and safe
is the new rule of this growing niche market.
Who can be sure of the extent of GMOs infiltration?
Advocate large compensation for accidental chemical spray drift
The organic farmer and rancher will soon become our rock star
Their hollywood-like studios will be the organic certified acres
which have been in the family for many generations
May the day when we appreciate our food producers come soon!

The Walls of Jerusalem, The Walls Of Fresno

A testament to a grand vision,
An awesome relic of the past architectural designs
Or a monument to the ideals of grandeur
Of an agricultural city and its proud people
What was it then? What is it now? A wall of fame?
A Central Valley-based temple to education and
The community college system in California
It's a benchmark of the State Center Community
College district and a plaque of honor to teachers
As well as students who filled her early classes
It's a witness to the visceral changes, sprawl of Fresno,
And the flight to anywhere north. Uncontrolled growth
Will ultimately hit the nearby hills and mountains
After using up precious and fertile farmland
Though battered by weather and hard economic times,
The Old Administration Building at Fresno City College
Never lost faith in her sense of historic value and inspiration
Her ivy-covered brick walls withstood the rough passage
Of Times, changing architectural tastes, and financial woes
This historic landmark is being renovated by
Her fans and The Fresno Historical Society
It's time to go retro and renovate our old buildings
It's time to celebrate the return to common sense
For all great cities with a vibrant downtown area
Invest in the renovation of their landmark treasures
Think about Sacramento, Berkeley, and San Francisco
May this newfound enlightenment and urban renewal
Find their way to the confines of Armeniantown,
Germantown, Chinatown, and West Side!
The new does not always have to replace the old
Go to France, Italy, Hungary, Germany, and England,
Be in awe of the beauty of old architectures
Adorning the cityscape. Tourists flock there to spend hard cash
Travel to New Orleans, Louisiana, North and South Carolinas
Realize the time-tested beauty of the prairie mansions
Now that the building is being peeled off, secrets are revealed
Creeping fig or Ficus repens -not ivy- which climbs
The glass and walls is being removed from the historic college
With the hope it will grow back
What years of celebration this renovated building will bring
To the children and grandchildren of former teachers and students!
Fresno's tears will have not been shed in vain. All the dashed dreams
And unsuccessful efforts will have been things of the past!

Hypergraphia

Find time to live your dreams and meditate
Carve time out for your passions. Fulfillment is near
What do you put first? Family or job?
You need a job to care for your family
Yet, a family will always be there for you
when a job is no more
How long will you put your dream on hold
to provide for your family?
So many delayed dreams, postponed promises
have gone to the ether. Nada. Zil. Rien. Nothing
Is it selfish to make time for oneself?
Peace of mind and a recharged battery are
great benefits you can't buy despite your great wealth
Rejuvenate your spirit, lift your heart, and
make each day worthwhile and full of praise and achievements

Write about your observations of the human conditions
Write with a pen or a keyboard; write with a pencil
Write on the bus, train and airplane;
Take snapshots of life's moments; time flies
Project the images that live in your head
onto the computer screen
Write in notebooks; write on paper and tissues;
write at the restaurant, the bus stop, the train station;
write as a hobby or a job; inject passion into it
write to leave the legacy of your infectious joy
Write to heal a troubled spirit, ease a burden, create a smile
Write to draw a tear, force a smile
on the face of the homeless and the orphan
Never underestimate your power and passion
Write to create new hope, define life
Write to immortalize events; write to show the people
who till the soil, cultivate and harvest the fruits, vegetables
and other foods that fill our tables not only in our hometown
but also in far away places such as Japan, South Korea,
England and beyond. Get hit with hypergraphia,
an overwhelming desire to write all the time and anywhere
Do you get inspired to write in the middle of the night?
Do you have some writing pad by your bed?
Record your ideas. They are not cheap. They build the world

This Land Is Our Land

Fleeing the hustle and bustle of life in big cities,
losing the passion of what took them away from
their roots anchored in the central Valley orchards,
leading a life of illusions and broken promises and
having to say enough is enough, two young men
find new ways to marry agriculture with tourism
This combination will bring forth the continuity
of a long-standing tradition. Farming must adapt
to survive and evolve with consumers' awareness

To all those who want to reconnect with the earth,
the ancestral land and life on a farm, agritourism is
the new sustaining alternative, a mutually satisfying act
farmers and urbanites are rediscovering each other again
Every weekend, carloads and busloads of tourists are
visiting farms, orchards, groves, rangelands
and water canals all over California. They are beating
the boredom of city life. They want to expose their kids
to the places where their fruits are grown with love
Parents want to say thanks to farm and ranch owners,
growers and food processors, seed breeders and workers
who keep our food supply safe and bountiful

O such fine beauties rediscovered on the agritours
Never before have the eyes of these children surveyed
the large expanse of land dedicated to crop production
Never have they known that the succulent peach and
nectarines were picked, plucked off a branch, not the shelf
Never have they played behind the steering wheel of a tractor
Never have they played in an old school bus redesigned
to become an ag playpen loaded with fruit and vegetable toys
Never have they observed a glorious sunset over the horizon
Never have they watched and participated in the milking of a cow

O such innocence and delicacy in bottle feeding a brand new calf!
Never have the tourists opened a bail of hay to feed the dairy cows
whose heads are resting on the slots and cement slabs
Never have they looked them in the eyes to see their patience
Never have tasted the tender meat of the free-range chickens
that add a new life and meaning to the farm experience
Stressed-out city dwellers will participate in the experience of
growers, farmers and farm children who see plants grow around them
May more season-specific events get organized for the agritourists!

Such Delights of The Granadas

Red, big, juicy pomegranates barely hang
On the overloaded twigs
The trees can't support all their weight
They cover acres of the fertile landscape
In Parlier, Reedley, Fowler, and Kingsburg
I have not given up the melodic lines
Of the surrounding hills and the rich
Vegetation wildly scattered on the banks
Of the San Joaquin River
For the first time, my son is hiking with me
"Daddy, this is like a jungle here," he exclaimed.
"Let's not tell anybody about it. This is our jungle,"
He added as we were walking and meditating
Over the Fall transition and leafless fruit trees
The sun lays its warm nuzzle on our foreheads

Once we reach our picnic site,
We are pleasantly rewarded with birdsong,
Chocolate, coffee, and lots of pomegranates
My son enjoys squeezing, spitting out,
And munching the red kernels
High in antioxidants and packed with vitamin C,
Granadas are the Valley's apples
They nullify the effects of glucose at the same time
Their bright red skin is leathery and bitter-tasting
The juice gets squirted in my son's face
And stains his brand new t-shirt
Alice knows how to get to these pods
Without any accidents
Who can eat a pomegranate without
Having juice dripping all over one's hand?
We, consumers, have come to expect
The pomegranates of the Valley's growers
The way we expect the sun to come up
Not in spite of rain and clouds
But because of them
The bone-chilling cold and freezing Winter days
Make us home and welcome any signs of Spring
So during the metamorphosis, don't abandon
The renewal of all things beautiful

Pho Soup Fusion

Whatever you call it, but don't forget
That all cultures love the greatest fusion of all
A bowl of warm soup soothes and revives souls!
We are enjoying various fusions these days
Fusion of cultures, economies, markets, and forces
Such is the reality of the current global market
I prefer the fusion of languages, tastes and cuisines
Europeans, Africans, Native Americans, and others
Contributed to this American type of brew, pot pourri
We love so much. Is it like a Cappuccino, a mocha?
Okra is favored by the Africans. Please pass the gumbo
The Spanish brought roast kid and wheat flour
To the new world. Grapefruit is from the Antilles
Who does not remember a good beef stew with
onions, tomatoes, and all kinds of chiles?
How about Pho? Vietnamese soup offers its
Varieties of herbs to the pickiest ones among us
From California, Arizona, Colorado and New Mexico,
One can enjoy tamales, pozole, edible flowers, mole,
And other true Western cuisine favorites
The Aztecs, Incas, Navajo, Hopi, Anasazi and various other
Indigenous groups inhabiting the vast fertile lands of the West
Have long found the secrets to great feasts, survival and longevity
They had sent their love to the future
We proudly inherit their centuries of labor
O such conviviality! Bring the appetizers. Bring the soup
Celebrate with the guests. Dance, sing and forget the pain
In the end, it's up to us to pass it forward
For fusion is part of our spirit and genetic makeup
How long will I stay away from a simmering pot of soup?
How long will the beef scare last? Habit dictates appetites
How long will I support and sympathize with the beef industry?
How long will I stay away from my B-B-Q grill?
Spring heals the wounds caused by Winter.
Summer is just around the corner once more
Let anybody tell me that our beef supply is safe again
For I see the steers grazing on the local rangeland
On the feed lots, they get fed alfalfa grown in our areas
Fighting cattle rustling and bioterrorism becomes essential
To the survival and safeguarding of this western way of life
Cowboys and cowgirls are itching. Cattle operators are hurting
We, consumers, want our steaks, hamburgers, and beef stew
We want to stand by our ranchers who feed us the best cuts

All of a Sudden, Rapture

We suddenly realized that
Everything else was less important
Nothing else mattered much for the
Few seconds they lasted. O such fury!
We all became frozen in time.
No one is ever ready for the magnitude
Of such natural catastrophes
For sure, they occurred before 911
And will continue to occur in California
Wild fires, flash floods, and quakes are all we know
But we can never get used to their aftermath

How can we grasp the futility and scope
Of the losses in human lives and assets
It's like here yesterday, but gone now, right now
The 1994 Northridge quake is vivid on our minds
Who could live through that magnitude 6.7 quake?
Lift your eyes to the mountains and observe
The dirt raised by the constant shakes
Look to your right and left and run away
From the walls of fires. Run to safer grounds
Yet, not even a hair was missing from your head
Though the grounds shook under your feet
Your loved ones and you escaped with no scratch

Freeways, main arteries of Southern Calif.'s cities,
Laid collapsed or severely damaged
Trucks could not deliver their products to stores
The lucky truckers and drivers who heard
The news stayed put at the truck stops
Other drivers were not so fortunate
They plunged into the abyss, unable to
See that a freeway interchange
Right ahead had collapsed at 4:31
They had put their faith in the rock-solid
Building and safety of our freeway systems
Landmark institutions and $ multi-million homes
Lost their allure and market value in no time
Californians live with the faultlines that
Crisscross this romantic state
As if we accepted our ultimate fate
We live one day at a time as we enjoy the sun,
The rangeland, beaches, Yosemite, and other jewels

Abrahamic Promise

The Jew embraces the Gentile
Both recognize their lineage
In the desert, they can trace their
Ancestry to the One who was called to leave
Everything behind to start a long journey
Ecumenical, interfaith, religious pluralism, mixed marriages
Interracial, biracial, biracialism, two-religion families,
Mix-raced, multiracial, multifaith are modern coinage
They are discovery terms and expressions that bring us
Closer to the fulfillment of the long-awaited promise
Of brotherhood, harmony, and union. One we are indeed!
Farewell to the hypocrisy of the past social contracts
Farewell to the anti-miscegenation laws which
Favored only one group who called the shots
Yet, covert or exploited interracial unions begat
Biracial offspring even to the Founders of this nation
Farewell to Jim Crow and all evil systems oppressing
A man's own blood and family. Call him a deadbeat dad!
It's not time to save face and social position any longer
The scattered children are tired of living in the shadows
The Israelis break the bread of peace with
Their Palestinian brothers. Then they share the same tent
Of reconciliation and complete brotherhood.
O Jerusalem, let the angel of peace stop the bloodbath!
Let them realize what matters most as both groups
Are not foreign to suffering and tribulations
The museum of Tolerance presents powerful shows
Of the holocaust and past struggles of African-Americans
The pictures of Iraqi, Rwandan genocide victims and
Palestinian militants are archived in newsrooms database
Let the non-Jew have his bar mitzvah at the temple
His Muslim interracial parents will appreciate the gesture
After all, it's a rite of passage just like Quinceaneras
In the Hispanic culture
We have Christmas, Hanukkah, Kwanzaa,
And many ethnic, religious celebrations in the Valley
The Americans will wait for their Russian, Vietnamese
Or South American brides in the true practices of
Democracy, freedom of choice and association
Love can't ever be regulated any longer.
The Asian grooms will cherish their English brides
The Africans will freely pick their European sweethearts
The Indian immigrants will abolish all old-country

Divisive systems. Only America guarantees such a melting pot!
Differences of skin tone, facial features, wealth, and language
Should not matter any longer
We are all sons and daughters of Adam and Eve (Acts 17:26)
For we were alike before we were different
From the dirt we all came; to it we shall return some day
Then, the floods wiped out everyone
The gene pool was narrowed back down to Noah's family
The same human blood is running through our veins
Moses married an Ethiopian woman
His brother and sister, Aaron and Miriam, spoke
Against him. They found displeasure in his union
Miriam's skin was attacked with leprosy for 7 days
For her sharp tongue and criticism (Num.12:1-15)
Bringing diverse people together found approval

Autumn's Bare Limbs

Nothing to hide any longer
All the glory is ready to be revealed
No more fungi, no more pests
No more leaves to hide them either
Cast your eyes upon the vast farmland
And see the huge nakedness and sameness
In the Garden of Eden, Adam and Eve
Found some fig leaves to conceal
Their nakedness. The fruit trees
Of the Central Valley of California
Have no more leaves to hide their broken,
Dead, crooked, and diseased limbs
Fall in the San Joaquin Valley reveals all
It's the time when leaves fall from
The aristocratic peach, nectarine,
Apricot, almond, and plum trees
Nature lovers, ecologists, builders, and hikers
Won't find any more leaves to hide their secrets
Drive down Freeway 99 past the new developments
Spot the names of extinct orchards,
A new way to memorialize the spirit of the landscape
Like children, participate in the fun found
In the numerous soft piles of mattresses of leaves
Plunge into these leaf mounds
Feel free to hurl leaves into the air!
For a brief moment,
Forget about despair, difficult times and loss
Live in the moment; walk down the various
Rows of fruit trees overlooking the river
Stop from time to time to admire and enjoy
Pick up some of these confetti-like leaves
After three days of diminished sunlight,
The Central Valley had a beautiful day
Of sunshine. Hikers and snowboarders,
Bicyclists and nature lovers are on the trails
The farmworkers are not pruning diseased trees
Whose trunks show the marks of years of care
No need to soak their hand pruners, loppers and saw
They are pruning to allow in more sunlight
And improve air circulation
The growers prefer the broad vase-shaped form of their
Deciduous fruit trees. With high insurance premiums,
They want to cut down on accidents from falls

Climbing a tall ladder to harvest the crops is always risky
Sticks in the Land

Patience is a virtue that most food processors,
Fruit growers, and farmers ought to possess
Otherwise, how else will they endure the long wait?
For many weeks, they plan and get ready
For the planting season. Seeds, seedlings,
New bank loans and labor contracts are ready
Under the cover of darkness and GPS technology
They plow away whatever rough hardpan and clay
That constituted a barrier
They set up drip systems, dig irrigation ditches,
Level the uneven grounds, plant, irrigate,
Cultivate, and nurture the young plants
Frail and bare they are over many acres
But they are arranged in rows with such
Geometrical precision that will please
Most landscape architects and occasional tourists
Then, the farmer goes about taking care
Of other farming chores for many years
Till harvest time. Or so they thought!

The time it took to secure the required permits
And plow several acres of this fertile land
Will partially be lost for ever
But the passion of farming and producing great crops
For the local and international markets
Will never leave this fruit grower and packer's heart.
How great is his loss of the young plants
On this new farm along Freeway 99?
Cattle rustlers used to be whipped and hanged
In the Old West. Modern farmers face a new plague
If they don't lose a portion of the harvest to bad weather,
They'll lose it to thieves wanting to make quick bucks.
Under the cover of a foggy night, bands of ag thieves
Drive onto the new orange grove to pluck the plants
Out of the fresh and well-plowed earth
Only footsteps and empty holes are left behind
Ag vandalism and organized theft are common problems
In the vast lands of the Central Valley
Dashed are the dreams of this young farmer!
Gone are the hopes of his wife and her investments!
Yet, they'll still have to pay the bank and family loans
Tractors and other family farm artifacts are stolen
Over here on this small family farm

The remaining sticks grow into mature trees

Wine and Worms

Isn't Napa Valley known as the wine capital of California?
Have you not stopped by the many wineries for wine tasting
On your way to the coastal range?
Did you know that the San Joaquin Valley produced great wine?
Her vineyards are celebrated for their health and yield capacity
their strong roots and scarred stumps prostrate in the fog
Just know that you can taste nuts in Madera, Hanford, and Kerman too
Don't you sometimes stop by the roadside fruit stands
to purchase fresh strawberries, cherries, plums, oranges, kiwi,
peaches, nectarines, grapes, apricots, prunes, corn, pomelo, and more?
Don't you like taking the annual Blossom Trail going from
Fresno to Reedley through parts of Clovis and Sanger?
Just know there is more to see as you venture out into
Kingsburg, Madera, Fowler, Kings and Tulare counties
Have you ever noticed the various stages of bud development
On almond, peach, nectarine, apricot, plum, apple and pear limbs?
Start with the green tip, pink bud, popcorn and luminescent, full bloom
stages before getting to the petal fall
Can you differentiate between the full bloom stages of a peach,
apricot, pear and cherry trees?
The first white of the prune ends up leading to its bursting ball-size, popcorn stages
Just imagine what type of carpeting these fallen petals create acres after acres!
None of this natural decor would be possible without the true engineers
Of the ecosystem. Worms are responsible for tilling and transforming the soil.
They kill organisms that make our plants sick. They fight off diseases
and break down toxins. Long live Valley worms!
Can't you taste the wine? It has to do with the quality of soil where the grape is grown
Wine connoisseurs know the importance of the right plantation.
Earthworms get the hard work done for all the farmers, growers and winemakers,
Consumers will appreciate them more when they surface in their own compost

Influx of the Cheap Labor Pool

They are young and ready to work
Their eyes are full of hope and adventures
In the U.S. mega-cities
Their arms are as strong as oak tree trunks
They are enjoying the best years of their lives
They are also tired of being unproductive
And living in abject poverty and indignity
They don't want to be stuck there any more
So they've decided to make some move
They are leaving behind
Everything they ever knew and grew up with
These illegal immigrants had set out to find
Work and meaning to justify their existence
On the other side of the fence and river
Pregnant wives and girlfriends stay behind
Siblings and loan sharks bid farewell and good fortune
Yet, they will wait for the monthly remittances
Without which they will starve on their desolate land
Illegal and undocumented, nonetheless dreamers and
Dream creators for their sons' education and future!

From all over the world, young men and women
Are drawn to America for the chance to work hard
And contribute to this country and to their family
At the same time, California, Texas, Florida, New York,
Utah, Colorado profit. All of America reaps huge profits
From the risk-all, docile, hard work of illegal workers
The economy always comes out on top
Such is the realization of a former Governor of California and
The president of the United States of America
In two separate acts favoring and acknowledging undocumented
Workers in our fields, hotels, construction sites, and roads
It's time we care about the faces and hands of the ghosts
Who shuttle from fields to fields, states to states
To harvest our crops! About 1.2 million - 2.5 million
Wage-earning farmworkers who pay far more in payroll taxes
Which they won't collect in benefits due to their legal status

It's time we pay attention to those who brave all types
Of border-crossing danger to do what we refuse to do
They willingly accept to pick up after us
It's time we give a decent tip to the laundry workers
At our 4-star hotels in our tourist-friendly cities

Most of them are not here to receive a free ride and welfare
It's time we establish eye contact with the busboys and cooks
Serving our meals at our favorite restaurants
It's time we say hi to the construction workers
In our flaming-hot housing boom and development
One accident, a fall or a back problem is enough to
Wipe out his savings.

It's time we appreciate the low costs of foods, fruits,
Vegetables in the whole country.
Without the availability of the cheap labor, these Calif.,
Florida, Texas, Washington State, New Mexico delights
Would be rotten in the fields.
It's time we give a better treatment to our nannies
Without them, there would not be two-income families
Child Protective Services would drag us to courts
We would lose the custody of our precious toddlers
It's time we protect our taxi drivers
For without them, the tourism industry would suffer
Travelers would be stuck at airports all over the country
It's time we acknowledge the presence of our gardeners
Without them, our lawns would not be cut
It's high time that employers advocate for the engines
Of their lifestyle and incomes

Tell me something now
What would we do without these workers
In the large fields of California and service industries
Such as meat-cutting, food service, poultry processing,
Ranches, orchards, daycare centers and construction?
We pay less to get more done
This way, we can afford to spend more
In our shopping sprees
The economy benefits. Everybody gets something

Freeway and Highway
Crosses

A swimming pool full of crosses,
Chocolates and special cookies
Day of the Dead or Dia de los Muertos!
Crash sites are all over the San Joaquin Valley
An electric pole here, a rock there,
And a tree trunk over there
The railroad tracks and our road system
Are silent, unpredictable and vicious killers
They are our necessary villains who deprive us
Of the presence of our loved ones
Amidst all the beauty of the Central Valley,
The rolling hills and fertile farmland,
Lie the public spots where loved ones perish
They become emotional and religious markers
For many residents too
The dense tule fog blanketing the flatlands,
The Valley floor claims its own series of crash victims
A brother, a sister, a cousin, a husband, a co-worker,
A father, a mother suddenly disappeared
In the darkest hours of the night or early morning
Broken windshield, marigold petals, fresh flowers,
Candles, tequila, tortillas de harina o de maiz
Tamales, cochinita al pibil, small crosses
Cajeta, moles, chocolate, frijoles borrachos, birria
And other treats favored by the departed souls
Are found all over the Valley
Dia de los muertos is celebrated
In the Hispanic culture. Others visit cemeteries
Surviving family members honor their dead
In ways that show perpetual connection and respect
Altars are erected in pre-selected corners of the house
Ofrendas, offerings of favorite foods, drinks, candies
Are displayed with lots of care
The dead is never too far away from the living
On special occasions, we clean the grave sites
Repair, and paint the tombstone,
Place a brand new bouquet or fresh roses,
Recollect and reminisce in
Graveyard vigil
Anywhere you go around the Valley,
You'll run into crosses and flowers

They are potent reminders that somebody,
A loved one once lived
On the altar, the living will continue to light a candle
For all the loved ones who have passed on
Day of the Dead is a celebration of life.
The bread and flower vendors hope to sell more
Family members will get inspired and courageous
Such is living, a continuum of births and deaths,
Gains and losses, abundance and scarcity,
Joy and pain!

Decadence

Nearly deserted cities, boarded stores
Vacant shops, dilapidated houses,
Drug-infested apartment complexes
With dirty syringes in the playground,
Meth cookoff and botox parties are
Like cocktail socials. Road rage, crack,
Random shooting, homicides, murder,
And cocaine are signs of the personal decadence
Such is not only the lot of the West Side,
Lying on the other side of the railroad tracks,
But it's also the measure of indifference
And low quality of life seen by some as a crime
Real Estate discrimination is ongoing
Others know you by your zip code
Which tells so much about your earning potential
In the land of plenty, how can we close our eyes
On a major sector of the population who is
Left to rot in the abyss of despair and poverty
Most talk about San Francisco as the only city
With a major homeless epidemic
Visit any major city and observe the homeless
At the intersection of major streets
Creating a ripple effect on the calm, aquamarine
Water, disintegration may reach each one of us
It's time to reclaim what justly belongs to us all
It's time to reclaim our parks that are infested by
Seasonal illegal substance growers with big guns
It's time to take our foods out of the earth
While protecting it for future generations
Such is the antithesis to degradation and desolation
Let the Valley landscape take one more deep breath
May the Williamson Act continue to give tax breaks
To landowners who don't develop their properties
A great number of them may seek refuge in chapter 12
A landless and equipmentless farmer is like a bird
Without feather in the dead of Winter

Superb Bowl or Super Bowl Hyperbole

Some say it's too much crass commercialism
Others are in it for the beer, male bikini waxes
cars, trucks, and erectile dysfunction ads
It's not only the crowning of a football championship
It's also a day reserved to celebrate and glorify consumption,
the good things and pleasures of American civilization
More tailgate parties, more barbeque, more garage get-togethers,
more chilli, more plasma tv sets, dip and guacamole!
Super Bowl halftime show for more than 90 million viewers,
Eyeballs marketers rely on to introduce their new products
Nothing is free; such is the current state of business
Everything is programmed to create more talk
Around office water coolers the next day
Expect to be shocked by sale pitches for bustier, bras
And underwear. Why such an uproar over a mammary gland?
A frown here, a kiss over there, and other unbecoming antics
Are all part of the biggest show on earth
Halftime show once becomes synonymous with lack of sensibility,
sex-simulating dance to highly suggestive lyrics with
The culmination of scantily clad performers baring it all
Before an audience of all ages. Young men's new haven!
It's a race to grab attention to introduce more products
Keeping one's name on the air and the buyer's mouth
Is the current norm, the new way of doing things
Super Bowl and its halftime show are new product galleries
In the consumer culture, they are featured below Christmas
How about Halloween, Easter, 4th of July, Memorial day?
Make each day a holiday from now on.
What's tasteless, tacky, and prudish is recycled once more
Will a bare breast cause the decline of the American civilization?

Every Inch and Each Act

Work never stops on a farm or a ranch
Prayers for more rainfall never stop either
With hundreds of heads of cattle to feed and
Move to fresh and green pastures, the work is non-stop
Like past seasons, the grass of the rangeland is already brown
This time of the year. The Summer months,
Recent winds and drought Have already sucked
The moisture out of the mountains slopes
From the rolling hills of Paso Robles to the oil-rich
Mountains of Coalinga and Bakersfield, CA.,
Many ranchers, cattle producers and feedlot managers
Are compelled to start buying hay. Their own hay
Production is insufficient. The seeds did not find
Enough rain to germinate
It's time to deliver calves, clean their feeding areas
It's also time to get ready for the branding season,
An annual ritual but a rite of passage for these calves
More expertise and special equipments are needed;
They are brought to the ranch from far away
There is never a sufficient group of helping hands
What a traffic jam! The ranch is teeming with activities
Crews of cowboys and cowgirls are coming and going
Some are excited to participate in this year's branding
Others are city folks who have arrived for the entertainment
Among them, you'll find the so proud veterans
Who can't wait to get the job done once more
They have the many years of experience to fall back on
They reminisce over past branding seasons
When pecan, walnut, chestnut, almond, peach, nectarine,
Plum tree stumps fueled the fire
How about branding pits as biomass alternatives?
Affordable co-generation companies need to be created

Unlike city dwellers who pay to discard their urban waste
Dairy farmers, fruit growers and ranchers are in a bind
When it comes to dealing with their farming waste
SB 705 sets a deadline for new disposal devices
Like their mothers, these calves will be branded
Hot sticks, special torches or iron that have become
Symbols of this family's farming tradition
Will get the job done. The cries and moans are deep
The flames from the pits are healthy
Formerly used to punish and identify criminals
And slaves, they were often used on cattle
To show ownership until a new era of greater awareness
Ranchers are adaptable business people who are quick
To lose non-productive and old practices
O such cruelty to a living skin! Advocacy and
Push to use electronic tags is the norm of the day
Consumers want fresh and tender meat. They are kings.
A mark of disgrace or stigma that won't sit well
With open-range-raised and organic cattle!
Tagging to improve the safety of the beef industry
And remove the stressors from these generous animals
Appears to be the way of the future
Drastic measures have to be taken due to the lack of rain
The ranchers can't afford to lose any more money
Buying hay is an expensive enterprise
When the drought extends its fatal grip
Fortunately, the culling season is just around the corner
What a great opportunity to cut the numbers down
For all the ranchers of the state!
The healthiest steers will command a good price
On the open market.
Consumers will be satisfied and happy with
All the hours of care and sacrifice that
Ultimately produced this succulent meal

May we order more steaks!
Let the barbecue season get started soon!

Island Figs

Pushed to a small corner of the road
And sandwiched between an old barn
and new housing subdivisions,
These fig trees are fighting for their last breath
Gone are the days when fig trees were
The carpeting masters of the Central Valley agriculture
But nobody can forget the fragile ripeness and
Delicious sweetness of these Summer and Fall treats
They take over your taste buds
In a matter of seconds and for a pleasant surprise
These days, the fields are immortalized by
The upscale shopping centers and housing developments
Bearing the names of the fiber-rich fruit
Just like the old buildings we bulldoze, we are destroying
The link to the agricultural wisdom of the past.
Yet, capitalism and civilization stand for a forward stance
A true sign of hope and a necessary tribute to the farmland
By the sons, daughters and grandchildren of those
Who labored arduously in the hardpan soil of the Valley
Are present in the selection of shopping
Center and housing names
In Fresno, most know Forkner as a street name
How many new residents know about his contributions?
Others enjoy going shopping at the chic Fig Garden Village
Stores and business centers. Tourists only like the great deals
Owning a piece of such real estate is the ultimate prize
And rewards for a few fortunate souls
Eating fig-based cookies is their only liaison to the generous land
An old man who can remember the boundaries of the city
sighs as he gazes around him. Slowly, he walks away and disappears
Among the new homes and traffic beyond the railroad tracks
 Pulled-out, yanked from the earth, the fig trees
Of this field have long ceased to produce great fruits
One can only wonder what's going to take their place
For a long time in the history of this changing landscape?

Firefighters and the Big One

Apocalypse as in the Revelations
Times of high tribulations and torment
Not the kind of man-made terror attack
That was inflicted upon the US and the world
But the type of event that will bring forth
A new day, new values, rapture
Renaissance and eternity
Yet, an adventure spirit, hedonism, and stoicism
Permeate across the land
They remain the main characteristics
Of most Californians who see the Big one
As the last frontier. Readiness and survival
Are the words of the day, les mots du jour,
Las palabras del dia
Let the good times roll! That's if you don't mind!
Be merry in these days while borrowing against
Future generations who'll have to worry
About paying back on the accumulated debt
They'll be burdened to repair our massive damages
Caused by our free-spending lifestyles
Why would anybody put up with living with
Tornadoes, hurricanes, carelessness, and avalanche?
That's what Californians would like to know
Blessed with year-round good weather,
We often forget our own natural calamities
The Hayward and Calaveras faults may be one
Who knows what's beneath our feet?
We may be dancing in the same plate!

It's just a sigh of relief for those living
On the East Coast to know
Nature, at times, cuts them some temporary slacks
The, they poke fun of our foibles, funny behaviors, antics,
The earthquake drills and kits
Our schoolchildren must have; underground shelters
Won't work around here. On the West Coast, there
Fires, started by lightning, that burn acres
Of lush land and expensive properties
Arson that breaks the hearts and devastate the hope
And dreams of hard-working men and women
Earthquake-induced fires that baffle brave firefighters
Who have to jump into hot zones, inferno areas

To rescue pets and protect a stable whose residents
Are frightened by the impending and sure danger
The horses are set loose to roam over the land once more
Full of adrenaline, they think about others' protection first
They appear to have no worry about their own peril and loss
As they jump into the heat, right into hell's mouth
Smoke jumpers, new heroes in the line of duty, dig fire lines
Carrying heavy loads to reach under-fires, they climb
Hills and mountains. They dance and draw the parameters
They fight against the oncoming waves of dark and gray
Flames rising from the canyon floor
On the other side of the deserted road

Parents continue to reassure their kids
In complete defiance of the natural threats
Of catastrophe and disaster. Complete chaos!
Tomorrow will bring a better day. Forget today
Hope and the expectations of the next frontier
Are synonymous
Though they may seek temporary refuge,
Westerners and Easterners will continue to
Live off the land. They will rebuild on the same spot
They will put the pieces back together and move on
San Francisco, Florida coast, Humbolt county,
Los Angeles Area, Coalinga, California's Central Coast
Rose again from the ashes and floods
Firefighters will return to their station
To polish their readiness skills and response tactics
Seismologists, weather people, business people
Parents and teachers will pay attention to reports
About the various fault lines and hectic weather patterns
A dove will be released to bring back good news
Of life and dry land in the nearby communities
The cherished plants of the Valley will survive
If not, a twig will be found
Survivors will pool together their courage, techniques,
And scarce resources to move forward
They'll jump to the help of the grieving elderly neighbor,
Orphaned children, homeless people and refugees
In their midst. The same way the indigenous dwellers
Of this land had sent their love to the present
Open hearts will replace open and damp grounds
It will be day of the rejection of self-interests
and current pessimistic values
True love and complete community spirit
Will be promoted without any reserves

Cry Over Manzanar

The American promise shall never fail anyone
despite the passage of times and hardened hearts
a harvest of shame was ultimately stopped.
In 1942, Fresno County, the most fertile and
richest agricultural area in the nation, saw her own
children ripped out of her heart. The rippling
effects of the Pearl Harbor attack touched
specific residents from the coast to the interior.
the country was at war. Fueled by inflamed
racism, drastic measures were taken.
the morale of these acts was later questioned
when all heads became calm and rational again in 1946
correction through restitution payments
and a language of remorse came to light thereafter
what a cleansing move for the collective soul!
sooner or later, the nation can redress her wrongs
first evacuees along Highway 99, Kingsburg, Selma
and Fowler, the Japanese American citizens were
sent to the barrens with whatever they could carry
they became internees in the rangeland and wastelands
O Manzanar, cry! O Fresno County, cry for your displaced children!
may they find redemption and acceptance like the prodigal son
cry over all those who are excommunicated in the Pacific Coasts!
the Civilian exclusion Order No. 34 impact was real
so was The Internment Order 9066. Shed your tears like watershed
that blesses and produces the bounty and beauty of the whole Valley
citizenship is not only a scrap of paper. Hurry up, Proclamation 2714
Manzanar dirt was as real as the Great Plains Dust Bowl.
like the Colored, Blacks or African Americans, the European Jews,
the Native Americans who were relocated to Oklahoma wastelands,
the Japanese Americans became the new children of pain
The legacy and memories of the Armenian and Rwandan genocides,
Haitian and Argentinian disappearances are
as vivid as those of the holocaust, terrorist mass killings,
Slavery, the dark smoke billows , sheets of dust and flames
Emanating from the fallen towers. Their marks will survive in history
They cried over the losses of their homes, businesses and cropland
they cried over their new pariah status in the heat and fetid fine dirt
at Manzanar. They became enemy taint, denizen and undesirables
while war may be necessary at times, men should prefer peace
then, they cried over the loss of mercy, compassion, plain decency
rationality, common sense, humanity and brotherhood

for the first time, African Americans were free to flee the vestiges
of slavery and Jim Crow in the Southern states.
their labor became most wanted in the West. Through word of mouth,
they got the good news. San Francisco soon had a new Harlem
for the war efforts, Blacks and Whites were working side by side
workplace integration, but not without any animosities!
With lots of on-going work, hope tends to lie in the future

Open-field Nuts Check

The glorious days of small rural family farms
Are becoming more and more fleeting
The threats of disappearance are real in California
There must be new ways to sustain the romance
Of living off such farms with dignity and joy
Chris and Trista's farming dreams were almost dashed
By low prices and oversupply of their harvested crops
The money is not in grape any longer. Crop rotation!
Their only hope lies in the fields of almonds they grow
They have managed to pay down some of the bank loans
They are safe for one more year! Almond prices are good
A temporary bright spot shines in the dark skies
Of the Valley's agriculture. It takes lots of money to farm,
Even much more to make money these days!
Fortunately, nuts are great for your health.
More snacks of dry roasted peanuts, almonds, cashews,
Mixed nuts, seasoned walnuts, and pecans
Are needed on our store shelves
"Eliminate the risks of heart disease, diabetes, and
Parkinson's Disease with those nuts," Harvard studies show.
Feel free to go nuts about CA-grown nuts!

On this overcast December day,
They are visiting their Kerman, CA farms
With two dogs and two boys in tow
Some of their workers are through
Pruning their Hanford fields
Another crew is ready to herbicide them
Daunting tasks await these pruning workers
In Kerman. More money to go to payroll!
Pruning shears in hands and tall ladders,
Workers move around with great precision
Acres of almond trees will have to be pruned soon
In a matter of days, mountains of waste woods
Are collected all over the damp rows.
Chris is already worried that some day he won't be
Allowed to have these pruning wastes burned.
SB 705 is phasing out open-field burning till 2010
Great acts to control pollution
And avoid the worsening of the local air quality
Farmers also care about the air quality and health of

Their own family members and consumers
They are working with clean-air advocates and
Air-quality officials who want a better quality
Of life for the residents of the Valley
"What should we do?" asked Trista, pensively.
"This is our livelihood. We are connected to the land
We can't just pack up and leave the farm. That's all we know."
"I read somewhere that the Valley is the second-most
Polluted place in the country behind Los Angeles."
Trista is a fourth-generation farmer. She remembers
The days when she used to accompany her parents
To the various family farms. Never a second thought
To burn the farm wastes. Huge, hot fires with sparks!

Trista is wondering whether her grandchildren will have
A farm to visit some day. May that day never come!
Burning is cheaper than chipping woods
There's so much money to go to the chipping machines
Biomass establishments can accept a limited amount
Of farm waste without an infusion of government funds
"There is no greater joy for my wife and me to continue
Doing what we do best. We grow fruits that feed the
Hungry in this country and around the world."
Trista walks away to check the trunk of an almond tree
"Farming has been a family tradition for so long. I would
Hate to see our fruits come from places like China, Chile
Year-round. The regulations may be hard, but these nuts
Are safe to our consumers."
Chris and Trista take comfort in the enhanced education
And consumption of these healthy products from their farms

Half-life of Parents

In times of war and peace,
Parents have some important work to do
They are raising the men and women
Of the next generation. Society needs them
The snapshots and films of their lives
File before us all

Half-eaten breakfasts, lunches and dinners
Multitasking parents are good at juggling
Activities, chores, homework and rides to
Baseball, basketball, football, dance
And Soccer practices
No time to have a good rest. No "me" time!
No more luxury of one's own time any longer
Raising kids causes parents to be always on the go
Parents are living through and for their children now
No more time for two any longer; no more time for
A private dinner; no more date on the town any longer
Intimacy and private talks have long died
We become part of the public and remain
Connected with public agencies, doctors, and
Other parents whose life is happily cut in half

Soccer moms hop in and out of their sleek vans
Half-eaten lunches on the road; frequent stops
At drive-thru restaurants, shopping stores
And coffee shops' restrooms
Pollution, fatigue, stress, smog and fog take a toll
On everybody's quality of life
Amidst the noise of commute, the loud music from the van's
Stereos, and the thoughts of caring for the loved ones
Left behind, a cell phone connects all the family members
Such is the condition of a working family with kids
With extracurricular activities

A new breed of domestic dads quickly learn
To socialized at the local parks, malls, bookstores
School meetings and various coffee houses
What greater joy to experience than that
Of well-fed, tired and happy kids tucked into bed
After a day of play, one or two stories?
It's time to have a few so-called personal minutes

Before thinking about the next day's errands
Maybe it's time to make a phone call and read a book
Even our sleep is never too deep
No wonder we get up tired and in need of a cup of coffee
It's the dawn of a new day and new hope
It's a chase of time. Parents bet how much
Can get done on this specific day
The piles of laundry can't wait
Neither can today's dinner
All parents need respite

Harvest Display

On a clear Summer day,
A family is braving
The heat radiating from the concrete
At the edge of the parking lot
Father, mother, son and daughter are
Searching for the exotic organic,
Ripe and juicy nectarines and peaches
They want fresh produce grown only
By the expertise of our Valley growers
So they arrive early in the morning
They want to support hard-working farmers
Who grow what they are selling
If they want good deals, they'll wait till
The end of the day, at market's closing time
At this certified Farmer's market,
There's some guarantee that the fruits
Will taste better than those found
At the local supermarket. At least, that's the hope!
The market's manager checks the certificates
No fraudulent vendor trying to sneak in here!
No phony homegrown produce sold at a higher price!
Fresh air and daylight abound always
No need to go to the hermetic,
Air-conditioned confines of box stores
No peddling is allowed on these hallowed grounds
Certified farmers offer free samples to all the shoppers
Who can't resist the positive assaults to
Their nostrils and taste buds
They become very trusted local heroes
Trust is at the basis of what they are doing
They can't afford to deceive these shoppers
Who walk around, tasting and comparing exotic produce
The kids ask questions and point their fingers
At odd-looking crops, vegetables, and berries
While parents are chatting with the growers
By the counter under the yellow stall
They are placing their pre-order of cherished items
That will be harvested and packaged with care
And especially for them
What a way to beat the crowd! Bribing has its place!
The organic farmer becomes a hero
Who will be invited to lunch.

Harvesting Delights
Of The Garden

Fall Transition
in the California Garden

Step into the garden
To enjoy its silence
A place of meditation
And recollection
Fall is near
Soon leaves will fall
From the trees
They will undress
To conserve and store
Nutrients, sap down to the roots
Make plans to take in
This beautiful scenery
Once for all

Fall is the time to go camping
The time to follow Football
And Soccer games,
Our kids' rites of passage
It's going back to school and
Tailgating, barbecuing, getting
Close to loved ones
The leaves will soon roll up to fall
And gather at the trunk
They'll begin their fall from Summer grace
Get ready to enjoy the change of season
Be part of this colorful transition
Winter is announcing itself; it's around
The corner. With fanfare and expensive decors
There'll be holidays to celebrate and trips to take
Fall is the time to get out
After a few hot Summer months
It's time to play with the kids on the grass
Soon to be covered with piles of leaves
Ah! Long memories of past Falls
In the East of the USA and California!
Each year, the Fall foliage continues
To create wonders and astonish us
With their beautiful designs

Long gone is Summer
When we simmered

Are we going to whine from the next Winter?
May the Fall days stay around longer!
Special fairs and celebrations to attend
Busy people to watch; lots of gift lists to make
Fall asks us to reconnect and
Take in the exterior peace and beauty of nature

Odes to Kings River

There would not be any harvest
Without the gift of your precious liquid

The Valley would be just
Another arid patch of land
Mojave and Joshua Tree parks
Would be better off

You never gripe even though we suffocate you
With trash, used tires, and other debris
You continue to be generous
despite our acts that dry your bed in some areas

You irrigate more farmland than any other river
We all depend on you for our food production

We promise to keep pesticides
Away from your banks
We want to keep you free
from any hubris and old cars

May all the tributaries continue to feed you
Roll on, Kings River! Rush down the mountains!

Liquid Gold, Sierra Snowpack

Where does our water come from?
How come our arid landscape is so productive?
Cast your eyes upon the mountain peaks
And observe the long stretch of white powder
From the weather precipitations falls solid rain
That announces the start of the ski season
Farmers and various users of this precious
Natural gift find their new source of enthusiasm
Gaze upon the mountains of the Sierra Nevada
Stay in awe of the beauty and majesty of the
Rich diversity of the rugged canyon country
Men's superiority is reduced to nil when stuck there
Yet, to our enjoyment and domination it was all given

Life resides in the snowpack of the Sierra
Far from its outlining reservoirs, life will be affirmed
The various seeds of the Valley are waiting
For the Summer snowmelt. Water will rush down
The mountain slopes and fill our intricate canal networks
New life will be created, nurtured and cultivated
In Southern and Northern California homes and fields
Lift up your head to the southern Sierra snowfield
Cast your gaze upon the northern Sierra snowpack
Realize that the San Joaquin and Kings rivers won't
Dash the hopes of the various water projects that
Manage and supply water to our courageous crop growers
High culture would be rendered insignificant in
Los Angeles and San Francisco without this liquid flow

How can we keep this scenic wonder for future generations?
John Muir, the Sierra Club, ranchers and like-minded
Individuals are investing in sustainability and stewardship
The survival of our ecosystems depends on our collective efforts
Likewise, the solutions to our economic problems
Reside in the ground. From the Great Depression era, we learned
To conserve and tap into our wild sources of energy
The nation's visionaries and engineers created a master plan
The New Deal's engineers set out to reign in our precious liquid
In the 1930s, construction on the Hoover Dam got started
From their historic desert status to the lively cities and fruit orchards ,
Las Vegas and parts of California have thus changed for good
All over the West, engineering efforts to store our water for
Irrigation and drinking show the can-do-attitude of our people

Think about Glen Canyon Dam and resulting Lake Powell
The Colorado River is to the West what air is to human beings
Likewise, dams are to America what Eiffel tower is to France
O such temples to men's engineering power, ingenuity and technology!
Take a look at Grand Coulee Dam, Friant Dam, Millerton Lake,
Folsom Dam and realize the grand vision and designs of the builders
Just like the indigenous people inhabiting this lush landscape,
FDR and engineering teams sent their love to the future

How can we pass this natural treasure forward?
Once a desert land, the central San Joaquin Valley got
Transformed into a green, fruit-producing ecosystem
Thanks to the Pine Flat Dam and the San Joaquin River
Let the cold, clear water roll down from those high mountains
Let our local farmers use it to continue growing our fruits
For we can't entrust our belly with others' growing regulations
Some day, the salmons, eagles, and waterfowls will fly again
In the meantime, let's enjoy kayaking, wakeboarding, snorkeling,
Fishing, hiking, exploring the various river systems, side canyons,
Waterfalls, pools, lush vegetation and diverse wildlife
Summer is just around the corner. These bodies of water become
The new paradises for jet-skiers, houseboaters, anglers, week-end
Fishermen and Valley residents
It's time to take stock of our assets. During times of calamity,
We are able to create great projects causing visceral changes
To our society, political landscape and topography
Despite increasing problems, the Bureau of Reclamation
Various state and private water agencies make the Valley
What it is today, the most fertile farmland in the world
They make California the $ multibillion agriculture industry too
Once for all, future generations will know that men and women
With great leadership and vision once interacted with and stood
On these hallowed grounds. The sweats from their forehead
Designed the water projects that blessed
And bathed the land in a sea of delicious and healthy crops

Lite Lit Bites

Lite is the antithesis of loaded, full, heavy, fully loaded,
Long-lasting, strenuous, dragging, beating-around the bush,
Spread over many pages a la magazine full of ads
Make it lite as in the case of lite breakfast, lite lunch, lite dinner
Lite meals can be synonymous with meals-on-the-go
With some lite extras such as lite French fries and lite sodas
We are not talking about home-cooked meals here
We have enough lite junks to clutter our way to misery,
Chronic diseases, obesity, expensive insurance, and death
We have lite beer, lite cigarettes, lite music, and lite work
How about lite ads during a long presentation?
Make the ads lite during the Sunday morning football games
Otherwise, we'll zap them with our ad-zapping devices
For that matter, make our movies and theater ad-free!
Make them even liter during the Superbowl and food fest
Macaroni and Cheese, ice cream, guacamole, chili beans,
Hot dogs are lite comfort foods
Most Americans like in hectic times.
How about some light chocolate cookies?
Chocolate is a vegetable after all. Good excuse!
A lite reader is not like a traditional one
He can pay enough attention to 30-second ads, very short
Stories and brief articles loaded with graphics and pictures
Yet, he must get to the gist of these well-written stories
Within a few seconds
Otherwise, he'll dispatch them to the ether. Complete deletion
Is not something that truly exists with new forensics
Lite users in a fast and complex world.
Ease up on the gas pedals please!
It's always a race to reach the next stop light.
Why should you be concerned by all these lite consumers?
Because they are engineering a new revolution in taste and lifestyle
Hey, why not lite lit as in this poem?

The Good Life
Go Nuts! Will you?

From the bank to the grower's account,
From the farm to the processing plant,
From the workers' hands to the stores,
We, consumers, receive the best nuts of California
Pistachio lovers all over the world
Are lucky to know that their treats
Are produced in large quantities
on huge acres in Avenal, Hanford, Kingsburg, Madera,
Fresno, Colusa, Sutter counties and beyond
Tedious and intensive may be the labor
Put into their production
But, in the end, we are all winners
O such mobile, portable salty nuts!
We can take them to the ball game
Where we eat them in the bleachers
We can carry them in our pockets
And reach them whenever we want to
Either at school or church socials
What's a good pastime without nuts?
Whether we are having fun at our lakes, rivers
Mountains and playas, we need a few bags
Of the last gold nuggets of the golden state
Drive out into the various counties and stay
In awe of the abundance of crops
Like chestnut and almond trees, pistachio trees
Add depth and texture to the ever-changing
Face of the Valley
Unlike other crops whose life expectancy
Is measured by the marketplace price and demand,
Pistachio will find new lovers all over the world
Let the once-barren land of the San Joaquin Valley
Continue to be irrigated, weeded and harvested
May the nuts continue to feed us all
While we continue to crack the shells open,
The pistachio growers will be able to meet their bankers
A new season will bring more farmworkers who will be
Able to make money to care for their family left behind
There'll be new payrolls, pruning, irrigation and harvest
Once again in the blistering heat of the Valley
Keep stress at bay and protect your heart
Have a few nuts! Will you?
Be like Californians. It's time to go nuts over nuts!

Poetry Like Water

Poets, rappers and musicians
What should be your primary motivation?
Is it money, fame, status or materialism?
Why should there not be
A place for material possessions
Such as large rings, new fancy cars, boats,
Homes on the beach, and private library and jets?
These things may not bring happiness
After all, a shot of ego boost lasts for so long
What then pushes us to pin ourselves to a chair
And write in complete solitude and under pressure?
It must be the needs to share with the world
Our fears and interpretations of our shared space
After listening and observing, writing must occur
Why poetry instead of Rap?
Rappers make money using poetry
Why can't poets start rapping their poems?
Word is the poet's main craft
Whereas poetry is just a medium
To the rapper's music
Some say poetry and rapping are now
Mutually inclusive and financially rewarding
Yet, poets are at the mercy of the publisher
They dream about a nice publishing contract
Just like the rappers, they have ambitions
To reach success and complete their writing
By publishing with a decent publishing house
Both want an audience. They are status-oriented
People living in an omni-entertainment country
The poet may not hear his poetry on the radio
While the rapper's music invades all media
What's clear for both is that there's
A huge gulf between realities and expectations
No full-page ads in Rolling Stone, Source,
The New Yorker, L.A Times, New York Times,
The San Francisco Chronicles and industry magazines
No national book award nomination, no book parties
Dashed dreams! Soul-shattering disappointments!
Their lives are not changed by the contract in their hands
Reggae king, Bob Marley, was recognized while he was alive
And more so after his death.
Few writers make a living churning pages
The majority must work elsewhere to make ends meet
The writer can't even make a living,

Let alone get recognized in this crowd
He is a solitary specimen whose immediate
Rewards are his words and
The richness of his meditations
Art is truly a way of life, not a career
Poets find writing poetry is its own reward
Art for art's sake!

Roosting Marvels, Roosting Headache

Long, dark, rolling clouds cover the sky at sunset
They don't necessarily presage rainfall
Around here like they do in the Caribbean region
Flying in formation like the Super Hornets and
F-16 Jets from Lemoore and Fresno, CA, these creatures
appeared not to leave any space for errors
After their foraging journeys, crows and egrets from
the Central Valley fly back to their roost on the river bluffs
After going on long, important missions to distant shores,
pilots of these high-tech planes return them to their base too
Military aircraft fans and family members usually
wait for their landing for hours beyond the fence
A promise that is not broken. "On the wings of birds,
the scattered children of Israel will be brought back home...."

The green flaming trees of the Caribbean attract all kinds of birds
They are a birder's paradise. They make ecotourism possible
Their roosting areas are protected in some countries
The long-necked, long-beaked, flaming-red scarlet ibises
are the national birds of Trinidad
They have fans in the highest places too.
From all over the world, tourists and birders flock to watch them
Come to roost in the mangrove and swamps
In Haiti, they roost on the flaming trees bordering the shores
and nearby coconut and palm groves

Treat yourself to an evening anywhere in the San Joaquin Valley
Right before your very eyes, one of the wonders of Mother Nature
will take your breath away and cause you to meditate
Through genetic coding, sanctuaries along the way are remembered
Migratory crows take over a Central Valley town
in the midst of Winter
They are making life miserable for the residents of Madera, CA
They won't find any fans among those
whose buildings and cars are soiled by their droppings.
Over time, a black car can be painted white
No more safe place with these feathered migrants!
The crows leave for the surrounding fields before dawn
Just like the numerous field workers who live in
and on the outskirts of the town. They are hard-working
and thrifty. Thousands of them roost on the same perch to
prevent them from losing too much heat to the wintry cold

It's a constant fight to conserve energy
The dormant trees have no more sap traveling to the limb extremities
The leaves have long fallen. They are not there any longer
to hide the blemish, stains, and pollution of daily life.
Bird droppings have always been around.
They are beneficial to agriculture in the continuum of life and death
They do create a mess on the sidewalks and steps
leading to important buildings when their roost is right
in the heart and arteries of any city
Yet, as protected species, these crows have a right to be
Just like any other Madera residents
May new ecotourism ideas and self-protection interests
of both species give way to a peaceful co-habitation!
By the time solutions are found, Spring will be with us once more
The blossoms and buds will turn into leaves hiding any nakedness

Spirit Fog

The days and nights of rain have long gone
The weather precipitations surprised
Many tourists in the mountains where
Snow was falling abundantly
It lured the flatlands skiers and snowboarders
Who never thought about the perils of avalanche
Danger lurked at every turn
Of the treacherous mountain roads
The nights are getting colder and colder
Weather people are predicting freezing temperatures
Like ghosts taking long strides all over the land,
Always timely, fog is creeping back into our environment
As we drive to work, school, church and supermarkets,
We go in and out of it. It sometimes embraces us
For so long a time that we feel disoriented
Fog engulfs our car. We can barely see its hood
Unable to see the road and oncoming vehicles,
We drive by memory and faith.
Days become as impenetrable as the darkness
Of moonless nights
When dense tule fog hits the floor of the Valley
Gone are the regular landmarks, the fruit trees
We have come to love and depend on
Pruning crews work like ghosts. They sometimes have
To succumb to the rolling power of the fog
Criminals take advantage of the fog cover
And thumb their nose at police officers
"Catch me if you can see me."
The sheets of opaque mist make
Farmworkers invisible twice
Until the fog is burned off by noontime, you will not be able
To observe the herds of cattle grazing along the fences
And barbed wires.
The free-range, organic herds are the prizes of any ranchers
It's a miracle that most of us survive to see Spring

Tamales for the Holidays

Nothing is discarded for good
The corn mush is the masa
80 pounds of the stuff with 30 chickens!
The corn husk becomes a product
That is packaged, marketed and sold
Fort he preparation of tamales
The same can be said of the banana,
Papaya and grape leaves which are
Used in the preparations of delicious meals
By some ethnic groups
Preparing tamales is a well-established tradition
In the Hispanic culture
It's a labor of love, a gift straight from the heart
Of the women who get together to prepare them
Mother, daughters and grandchildren participate
In the ritual before the holidays
In the past, men used to hang out outside
Around the bonfire to enjoy a few favorite drinks
They joked, watched games, listened to music
Cooked, and sent the tamales
To the hungry female guests waiting inside the house
Never will I consume such a Tamales meal
Without remembering the intensive labor
Involving planning, shopping for ingredients,
Broth, Crisco, butter, mixing the masa,
Preparing chile and tasting to have the right accent
If your house is used as the site of preparation,
You'll lose access to the kitchen and dining table
The aromas of the spices and boiling chickens
Permeate every corner of the living room
Refuge can only found in the bedrooms
Or bathrooms behind closed doors
If you are truly aroma-averse,
Schedule to be out of the house until such
Times you suspect the women may slow down
The production line. They won't notice your absence.
Reminiscing about past Tamales productions
And family stories, the women talk, smile and laugh
Advice and instruction are metered out to the youngsters
Some workers prefer to stand up to work; others complain
About their inability to prepare dinner for their family
Celebrating Christmas is all about the work, togetherness,

Anticipation, gift wrapping, making lists of gift recipients, spirit,
And last-minute preparations that lead up to the day
Piles of chicken bones are everywhere. Constant cleanup is the order!
Large containers are full of meat mixtures and fillings that will be spread
On the corn husks which get rolled in a neat fashion
Then, the tamales are bagged and stored in the freezer
They'll soon be given away to friends and family members
What and exotic way to say "Happy Holidays to you!"

The Redeemer and The Redeemed

There is still time to join the table of reconciliation
Abandon your old ways and terror tactics
Forget about the legacy of the past
When you claimed your superiority over all and
Engaged in servile practices, exploitation, hatred,
Prejudice and discrimination
Let's send our love to the future
The present is ours. The past is our ancestors'
Let's be friends and brothers once more
Do not dwell on what made us invisible and
Indifferent to the visible pain and poverty of our soul
It's time to change our attitude
For the evil forces have formed a league against us

First and second world wars showed the wide range
Of our self-destructive powers. Mutually agreed Destruction,
Retaliation and self-instinct preservation
Became the word of the day
Then, Hitler and Mussolini came to the world stage
With their ideologies reeked of hatred and confusion
"Battle becomes the new condition of man," Mussolini said.
Pearl Harbor reminds us of the sacredness of any people's rights
The atomic bomb led to the wasteland of Hiroshima
Yet, we are interconnected as we are surfacing
For air in the swimming pool. The wind blows every which way
Let's not think about the realms of horror that stockpiles
Of the hydrogen bomb may cause to humankind
The deluge is already documented in the Bible. In it, lies our future
The heroes of past wars and conflicts are appealing to
World leadership to put an end to this arm race
They are compelling us to think about posterity
Let's deal with these daily problems: Pollution of air, water,
Oceans, upper atmosphere; the death of forests, of species,
The depletion of natural resources and essential minerals,
Overpopulation and threat of world famine,
Dislocation of entire peoples; and the apparent disintegration
Of structures of civilized order. Dictatorial regimes will fall.
Let's counter the immense evils of war with our awareness
And huge doses of pacifism. May we proceed with lots of
Acts of kindness, decency, pity, integrity,

Compassion and independent courage

California Outdoors Cooking

The Food Spring Cookoff

Settle back and relax. Every year, the show is on during the Spring season. We are all spectators watching the film of seasonal changes taking place. Waterfalls, flowers and a bubbling surprise await you in the comfort of your own property. Where else can all of this be happening? Let your imagination run wild in your back yard garden. Right on the deck by the swimming on the left, this is where we have our yearly rendez-vous with our Spring family grilling. With a cool breeze blowing from North to South, the smell of the chicken we are grilling this afternoon won't get my party all intoxicated. With so much energy to burn, the kids have never stopped using their scooters back and forth nearby. No matter what the sound of running waters tends to soothe my senses and nerves. Our backyard grilling is such a yearly rite of passage. It's something every member of the family is looking forward to. Even though the menu is a little bit different and diverse this year, most of us look forward to this moment with great anticipation.

Char-Broil Makes life easier in the back

For most of us, Spring would not be meaningful without all the time we are planning on spending outside. Either to shape up the front yard and plant some new flowers around the house or do some specific work in the garden, we all enjoy the coming of Spring. What would it be without getting this grill started? The Charbroil grill is easy to use. Just spend the time to get your ingredients ready and place them on the stainless steel burner. If you are preparing some hot dogs, you can place them on the top part. You can place the bowl containing the ingredients on the side burner if you don't choose to use it. If not, you can place them on the other side. This Char-Broil grill is easy to use and move to whatever location you want to. Just go ahead and load it up on the back of the pick/up and you are ready to hit the next gathering spot. I have found this grill to be very useful in the preparation of vegetables. My favorite thing to grill is fish. It handles almost everything we throw at it. The only thing that you will have to get after purchasing this grill is a tank of propane.

Features:

After your guests are long gone, you won't be stuck with a hard-to-clean grill. The Char-Broil is built up such that you can have easy access to the dirty components. Cleaning it was a breeze. The two buttons that are located right on the front of the grill are so big that you can't miss them. Just turn them to the right side and ignite your grill. If it's windy, you won't have to worry about scaring flair-ups. They seem to be limited. Keep in mind that they don't completely disappear. It's one of the hazards of outdoors cooking. Flair-ups will happen.

Recommendations

This grill can be used by anybody preparing foods for a medium-sized group. It will be fantastic in a family setting. I have watched its use in the feeding of a few tailgate parties at two local universities. The Red Wave of the Fresno State University can be spotted using it on a few occasions. If anything, this Char-Broil is great to have in one's backyard. It's reliable and fairly easy to use.

Summer Grilling in California

Ladies & Gentlemen, Family Chefs, Fire Your Grills This Time Again!

Are you craving for some outdoor-cooked, tasty meals this time of the year? Look no further than Charbroil 800 Big Easy Gas Grill to satisfy your hunger.

Who can resist the great outdoors these days with the beautiful weather of California this time of the year? If I can't talk for many of you, at least, I can talk for my family and those who are close to me. Besides going to our beautiful parks, river beds and the beach, we usually assemble on our porches and decks to enjoy either breakfast, lunch or dinner while watching the sunrise or sunset. May brings us so many occasions for all of us to be together, whether it's for Mother's Day, graduation ceremonies and Memorial Day.

With the blessing of long, sunny days, this week-end will see many of us hitting the road to our favorite camping grounds and coastal beach areas. So it makes sense that most of us will be eating out. For the past few days, I have been very busy shopping and cooking for a member of our extended family who was going to graduate from California State University-Fresno with a degree in Accountancy and Business Administration. It was time to prepare the foods, season the steak. It was barbecue time for what ended up being a large group of people. Obviously, I received assistance from the family members. But I was in charge of the food category. We put the family's newly purchased **Charbroil 8000 Big Easy Gas Grill to good use**. More than anything, on occasions such as these, one realizes the true importance of being family members. Since it's Memorial Day holiday, it's also time to think about those who passed away. But most of them will be with the rest of us in spirit.

Big Easy Gas Grill Is The Product of the world's leader in barbecue grills, CharBroil
There is no doubt that this company calls itself *the keeper of the flames*. It's quick to innovate and bring new products to the market. This year, it brings us CharBroil 8000 Big Easy Gas Grill in time for the holiday season. What's great about this new grill is its multi-functionality. It's easy to use it to prepare your breakfast, lunch and dinner.
Impressive Features of the Big Easy for you, guys!
Let's take a tour of the gas grill first

On the right front, you will find the fuel gage that tells you when the tank needs filling. There is no going at it by faith. No more blind spot! If you are cooking, you want to make sure you have enough gas to complete your cooking. Then, you will find the flush-mounted side burner which can serve as extra cook top or shelfspace. Now, this is very important in that it will come handy as you cook outside. Everything you need will close to your hands. Remember that this side burner is also found on the left side. Right below the side burner, you can see the tank which can be tilted to accommodate you better.

This gas grill is very stable thanks to its large, wide wheel base. The large wheel ensures a stable cart. Right in the front, you will see the condiments basket and towards the left side under the side burner, you will see the bonus side shelf which can double as storage. The moniker of Big Easy may stem from the fact that this gas grill is truly easy to use. Just take a look at the large grip knobs that you can use to get a clean start. That's the ignition knob. Then, another large knob controls the separate burners.

What can you cook with this grill?
How do you keep it clean

There is no doubt that you made a good choice buying this gas grill. In general, gas grills are very convenient, stay cleaner and are easy to control. They cause you less headache with mess and ashes to clean up or empty. The only thing is that if you don't have a natural gas installation, you will need to refill your LP tank.

You can use the porcelain cast iron griddle to prepare your eggs and pancakes or a grilled cheese sandwich. The porcelain cast iron deep dish can be used to prepare your stir fries and deep fry. The benefits you will reap from using the grill outside are that your house is going to remain fresh and clean. When it comes to using the rotisserie burner, you don't have to worry about a thing. It's placed above the main grid, allowing the grease to drain away for healthy cooking and avoid flares up.

Obviously over time and many uses, your cast iron grates will turn black. To clean them up, all you need to use is boiling water. It will get the job done.

What's the warranty package like?
Among all the good reasons to buy this gas grill is the warranty package:
Lifetime warranty on the casting
5 years on the burner
10 years on electronic ignition
1 year on all other parts.

Hey, you can always buy a new insurance or negotiate your way to a better one.

Combat hunger with the leader and keeper of the flames!

Do I Recommend this Gas Grill, Big Easy?
Yes, it's a good buy.

Teach Your Kids The Right Way, Your Values & Civic Lessons

If every parent felt responsible enough to take time to teach their children important civic values or their own values, we would have less trouble today. Alas! The kids are left to raise themselves while parents are busy trying to make ends meet. So far, they know they have to provide for their family and keep up the lifestyle. In this ever increasing commercialism, the battle to own and own more of the latest gadgets does not seem to end.

Most parents are caught up in this trap. This explains the growth of the childcare industry. Other people are raising other people's kids. They are learning others' values. With an overdose of TV watching, these kids are exposed to all kinds of ideas and foreign values. Having exposed some of the reasons for an apparent lack of teaching, I would like to propose a few ideas to help curb the uncomfortable level of violence preying on our precious little ones.

Remember that you don't have to blame yourself. There is nothing to be ashamed about. You are working hard to meet your goals and provide for your kids in this competitive society. The demands of the new economy may cause you to spend time away from your kids. Whenever possible, create time for them.

1. Show interests in your kids' hobbies. This way, you will have a chance to get to know them.
2. Choose the time when you can share your values carefully. Dinnertime may be a bonus for great communication.
3. Listen to your kids' stories, concerns, challenges, ups and downs. Sometimes, what it takes is to just listen to them.
4. Be diplomatic. Don't come down hard on them when their ideas or actions don't match yours. Redirect them and teach by example.
5. Learn to be firm in your decisions. Take your stance. You can teach important negotiation values.
6. Use common sense and reasoning. Appeal to their judgement and reasoning skills. Don't expect to be successful in the first few attempts. It may take some time depending on the kids...
7. Avoid falling into the habit of buying their favor. If they misbehave, they should already know what the consequence is going to be. Here, the premises are that there was some previous teaching or discussion of the house rules.
8. Be willing to give a second chance if you see that the kids can learn from their mistakes. Don't cut the allocations and car...etc..yet.
9. May your spouse and you become good role models. If you yell at each other in your kids' presence, you are sending out the wrong message. Argue politely. Listen to what the other has to say. Keep control of your emotions.
10. Monitor what they are doing, the type of friends they are hanging out with. Abuse of drugs, alcohol or any alcoholic beverages should be avoided as much as possible. Kids learn from parents. There should not be any excuses for behavior unbecoming good citizens. Discuss some of the tough, violence packed shows and games your kids may have been exposed to. Don't chicken out to give your opinions about them. This is how you can teach them your values.

These are just some points to mull over. Let's all do our part to stop this epidemic in our society now. Each one of us can contribute to the reduction of our children's killer...

Los Angeles and Jay Leno's Cars

The Los Angeles Renowned Car Culture

Pros
Temperate weather and lots of fun sites and expensive, gated communities
Cons
Heavy traffic and crowdedness

The Bottom Line
In Los Angeles, you will be ashamed if you don't own a car despite all the sidewalks at places such as Hollywood and Bel-Air...See it to believe it!

What do Jay Leno, ordinary Angelinos and famous Hollywood celebrities have in common? The love of cars runs deeply in this city. On any given day, the three-or four-lane freeways and highways leading into LA are crowded with vehicles of all types. You can see the Humvees and the other pricey autos filing in front of your eyes and carrying the stars to their destinations. By the way, most of these vehicles are chauffeured. Ordinary Angelinos do the same. They drive to the local Farmer's markets and the beach. Only in LA will you so many residents jump into their cars to go to any places. This may be one of the reasons nobody can't get anywhere.

The car culture

If you decide to drive 30 minutes south of Los Angeles, you will reach Huntington Beach. Besides the great surfing and tanned bodies, you will sure find a lot of model cars, some of them are retrofitted by ordinary residents with a taste of being different. Being different is one of the fundamental elements of the Lowrider culture, for example. In fact, Lowriders constitute a booming industry in the area as part of the established auto industry as represented by the likes of Mitsubishi and Toyota etc. On the beach, young guys just go crazy over the minute details, design and hydraulic performance these monster-like vehicle have. They make them dance, go as high as their power and gravity will allow. All of this comes with the appropriate attires of baggy clothes. If the owners of these automobiles are not there to surf or enjoy the ocean, most of the times, they are there to just show their toys to the public. When it comes to showing these cars, it takes a whole personality and atmosphere of its own. Beautiful, ordinary young women remain at the centers of these shows. They are often clad with string bikinis with which they are battling to cover some essential body parts. That's part of the show. A hot lowrider can't afford to be shown by a girl who does not want to show some skin! Some of these girls who claim to be models are often the car owner's girlfriends, spouses or family members. **So, don't go too crazy about them for fear of attracting some blows or fights**

LA as the entertainment capital of the world

Well, you are talking about a diverse place, you are talking about the showbiz capital, Hollywood. Cars are very important. How many movies have you seen without a car, a car chase or a couple having a relaxed time in a car? Cars are used as the extensions of the living room for most people. *How many of us who can't remember the last time we kissed our date in our car?*. No matter how many airplanes, copters are used in movies, cars are the most used in comparison. For many, becoming a car owner is an accompaniment of the self-entitled right to happiness and amass material goods. *This is why most people refuse to walk to any distance these days. Those who are compelled to walk around to run their errands or walk to work are often looked down upon in this city.*. It appears that the underlying idea is that one should not dare living in LA without owning a car.

How would anybody have fun in the fun capital with no cars?
Consider the amusement parks and other attractions
For sure, there is lots of entertainment to be had in LA.
* What do you make of Disneyland in Anaheim? Every year, millions of people come from all parts of the US and all over the world to recreate themselves at its many attractions. The Disney board of directors have just added a new component catering to adult visitors to the park. California Adventure will attract more visitors as its rides, hotels and restaurant get more popular.

* Knott's Berry Farm

* Magic Mountain for the thrillseekers of the world

* Universal studios

* Two National Basketball teams (The Lakers and Clippers). You see, one is not enough.

* The Los Angeles Zoo.

* Malibu

* Hollywood BLVD and Bel Air

* And the various Farmer's Markets, some of them have been around for a long time. For example, Grand Central Market has been around since 1917. **To go to any of these sites, one must drive. You can now understand why the roads are always crowded anywhere you want to go around the city. Tinseltown is a busy place with cars.**

I hope this article has shed some light on why it always seems to be so crowded in and around LA.

What's Special About California's Multiethnic, Multifaith, Multicultural Families

Love has no boundaries. Neither can it be regulated any longer. Anti-miscegenation hypocrisy gave birth to a special group of people despite the times. Many have tried to keep those divisive laws in place, but they failed miserably. Only their hypocrisy and inflamed stubbornness kept them going. We build obstacles and barriers in our life. A beautiful person is just beautiful irrelevant of his/her origin and makeup. For that matter, beauty does not transcend cultures. What's beautiful here in the US may not be in Brazil, Nigeria, Hong Kong or Argentina. People unite because of the chemistry, that little thing you can't pinpoint or explain. Look into the eyes of anybody who may be from anywhere in the world, you will know if there's attraction.

Unfortunately, we are the sum of our historical, cultural and familial heritage. We go into a relationship with all our backgrounds and stories. Unless we make a deliberate effort to distance ourselves from our fears of the human being, we may not feel comfortable enough with ourselves to extend love to somebody else. This is true in all types of relationships whether they were between people from the same culture or not.

This leads me to talk about some of the things that are going well in a multicultural family.

1. There is always the element of challenge. It is a constant learning process. There is so much to learn about each other's culture that it is never boring.
2. There is an element of full acceptance by both partners. It goes beyond love. Both partners accept to experience each other's life and culture.
3. Multicultural families want the same thing that all other families want out of life. They also want to pursue happiness and wealth.
4. In a lot of ways, multicultural relationships are not for the weak-hearted.
5. The expectations are high. In-laws and friends wonder what the kids are going to look like. They often predict these families won't make it or stick it out for long.

Some of the most important characteristics of multicultural families are the willingness to attempt new things, the exploration of new dimensions of their lives and the total trust to each other as they brave society's historical statistics.

Now, don't go around and say that you can't meet the prince charming. You have limited your resources and access. A good man or woman is a good one wherever they may come from, irrelevant of their status, financial position and even educational level. Be open-minded! The bond that unites multicultural families can not easily be broken. It is a deliberate choice to be together!

The Museum of Tolerance

Pros
Dramatic stories about the holocaust, Civil Rights Movement and other incidents

Cons
Words impact

The Bottom Line
If you want to challenge the intolerance and lack of sensitivity of some individuals, ask them to meet at the Museum of Tolerance in Los Angeles.

A few months ago, I visited **The Museum of Tolerance** for the very first time. I could not resist participating in this trip organized by my colleagues. For a number of years, I had been reading about the Simon Wiesenthal Center, its lectures and workshops that bring important speakers to reflect on various troubling issues of our times. As if trying to play hooky from work, we all agreed to take off on a Monday. So, early that day, we met at our rendez-vous site to catch the huge charter/tourist bus we had rented. Besides the normal daylilies and various other blooms that we expected to see on our way out the Central Valley of California, many of us made plans to bring our favorite movies to watch on the bus video system. What kind of bus will take us to Museum?

Can you imagine how disappointed we were when the driver announced that he had to change bus the very morning. The van that was assigned to him the night before became unoperational. He was then assigned this new one whose video system was not functioning. Then, he went on to try some humor. But it was clearly the wrong time to attempt to give us our requests. After all, the fees for the rental would remain the same. And, we had also planned to reward the driver for his good work, for spending the day with us. Well, most of us did not let this lack of equipment disturb us and take anything away from the lessons we expected to learn all throughout the day. At the end of the day, we did not take it on the driver himself; we ended up giving him a large tip.

What's the museum all about any way?
Part education, part history and multimedia, part drama, part showbiz

After a two-hour drive, we made it in front of this expansive brown building located at 9786 West Pico Boulevard. I was personally touched by the number of charter buses picking up or dropping young people in front of the building. We stepped out to find an agreeable weather, the kind that attracts many to Los Angeles. It was very temperate. It reminds me of some Caribbean islands with the only exception that a sea of heavy traffic waited for us there. It was at that moment that an apparently beautiful woman driving a Mercedes started pounding on the horn and wanted the pedestrians crossing over to the museum to hurry up. Groups of teenagers understood her sense of haste and took even longer to lift one or the other foot. They crossed lazily while talking to each other and on their cell phones. At one point, a buddy of mine thought she was going to accelerate her gas right through them. You should have seen her movements in the Mercedes that became blocked by another Charter bus, too long to turn to the right at once!

More than 350,000 people visit this museum. Among these visitors, you can find more than 110,000 children, school age kids coming from all over the state of California and beyond. I ended up meeting visitors who came in from other countries too. In fact, the Museum of Tolerance has attracted the powerful and the famous too. Prime ministers of

Israel visited it. King Hussein, Dalai Lama visited it too. Countless local stars have been to the museum. More than any other group, it's the young people, the professionals and ordinary men and women wanting to challenge their views and thoughts of others who continue to pour into this brown brick building in this somewhat economically depressed part of LA.

Everyone should be treated with respect and dignity
Beyond the physical characteristics such as skin color, we are all unified through DNA, at least 99.99&

While browsing the site the night before the trip, I read the following statement which made me think a lot.
"The museum is a high tech, hands experiential one focusing on two central themes: Dynamics of racism and prejudice in America and the History of the Holocaust which is the ultimate example of man's inhumanity to man." For our tour guide, we had a holocaust survivor himself who quickly took advantage of my height. He asked me to be his back anchor since other groups were following us. This way, when he saw me, he would know he had all of my group. I accepted to help this rather short and round old man who was very nice and knowledgeable about the holocaust. We soon found our way around a round circle that took us to the basement where the tour got started with a video that then summoned us to pick a door. The writings on the two doors were very meaningful. We entered through the door of Tolerance to be soon shocked by some racist 1950s' rhetoric spewing out of the microphones about black people, negroes. On the wall were written the various historical phases of the Civil Rights Movement. Then, we walked past the infamous Counter, a re-enactment of the sitting-in. That's the Point of View Diner which is a recreation of a 1950's diner with red booths that served a menu of controversial items. Members of other tours were there. We went straight into the next room to participate in an answer-question session that challenged us to think about the fate of women and children worldwide. They are being abused, mistreated, maimed, and exploited in various ways. Then we went through the wall of The Civil Rights Movement with the famous speech by Martin Luther King. Soon thereafter, it was time for us to get a card from a machine that was not too cooperating. The huge door opened onto the Holocaust.

By then, an old couple joined our tour group. The man appeared very troubled by some sites. He managed to answer a question asked by our survivor who questioned him about whether he was there. In unison, the couple answered that they had migrated to the US from Germany. They added that their parents died there. They had been to many of the sites such as Dachau etc. In the Holocaust section, visitors are led back in time to become witnesses to the events of WWII. I was so fortunate to have our tour guide who had lived through all these hard times! As we went through the tour, I grew closer and closer to those suffering in those violent times. The Survivor testimonies were touching. It's hard to go through all of this without being touched. It's the human side of this tour! We left the basement to go upstairs through the same circle. Be ready to walk. If you can't, they will provide you with a wheelchair. That's where we found the paraphernalia of the Nazi movement and the elements of torture and bed frames. If you have time, you can go on to the multimedia center.

The museum of Tolerance is open every day except Saturdays. Call 310.553.9036 or go to www.wiesenthal.com or motlc.wiesenthal.com to find more information or make a reservation.

I am happy I could go there to witness history. You will be able to become more tolerant of others no matter what their race, nationality, sex or sexual orientation, skin color and financial status or any other things were.

Tour Focus can be: Cultural diversity and awareness
Anybody, from the student to the professor, the college student to the homeless man, the professional to the unemployed, the social workers to the doctors can learn something new. On-going training is very helpful to promote sensitivity to any group of people.

Peach and Nectarine Bites

My two favorite stone fruits from the Central Valley of California

How would you like to bite into a juicy peach or its fuzzless cousin, nectarine? But first things first, have you ever wondered what keeps a farmer, a fruit grower motivated to produce the magnificent fruits we have come to appreciate all year long? For sure, it's not glamour. It's not the attraction of fabulous sums of money. It's not the immediate feedback they get from the consumers of their efforts. What is it then that keeps this strong breed of American farmers on the soil, weathering bad seasons, all kinds of regulations and permits, thefts as in fruit theft and cattle rustling, the prospects of poor returns and absorption of family farms by larger farming companies and many other risks? How about the new "burn day"

Farming can be lonely and financially unrewarding despite all the long hours of labor, decisions and loans. Traveling up and down the floor of the Central Valley of California, I have had the opportunity to visit many family farms and commercial farms. If anything is common to all these special people is their love for creation and improvement. They don't like to give up and show proof of leadership, creativity, innovation and courage. In a way, as an urban consumer, this is my privilege to inform them that their efforts to produce were not for nothing.

Pismo Beach, California Central Coast

In Brief:

Pros
Lots of activities to participate in; beautiful white sand and quaint shops and boutiques

Cons
sand-throwing wind

The Bottom Line:
If you are looking for a good holiday or vacation hole, Pismo Beach, located in Oceano, is a good destination. Check www.crackedcrab.com for the food

Just find your way to scenic Highway One if you are in California, you will undoubtedly hit Pismo Beach. Whether you want to visit it from Los Angeles or San Francisco, Highway One will take you right into the nice seaside, little town of Oceano. Just two weeks ago, I spent a day of retreat there with my colleagues. This was probably the 20th visit to this beautiful corner of the Central Coast. Whenever I get stung by the traveling bug, I take my family to Pismo State Beach to relax and play in the sand. With all the amenities it offers, it will stay on your mind for a long time after you've vacationed there. Pismo only has that kind of magic draw. Both the kids and your spouse will love it and pick it among many others.

First things first, how do the bathrooms look?

This should not be the least of your worries, folks

On your way to the town, you will see the crashing waves of the ocean on your side. All that does to you is to pique your interests in all the fun you will soon have. Shops and businesses catering to tourists and sea-goers line both sides of the highway. Then, if you are lucky enough or early enough, you may find a few unoccupied parking lots. Take them as soon as you can. In a heartbeat, the surfers and out-of-towners will arrive to occupy them. Passing the rustling of the leaves of the short palm trees, you will walk down to the pier. On your right, you will see the restroom. When I was there on my recent visit, the stalls were quite clean. I must add that we were there before noon time, even before the surfers arrived on the beach. I could count on one hand those who made out that day. Any way, there were enough toilet papers and seat covers around. The urinals were in good conditions. I soon exited the restroom to take a few nice pictures of my colleagues on the pier. I will report that I did not hear any complaints from the other members of the team. Both males and females were happy with their conditions.

Nearby hotels, motels, wildlife, volleyball and kites *Pismo Beach is a kid-friendly beach*

Pismo State Beach offers all kinds of attractions. You can make whatever you want of your stay at the beach. If you decide to stay there for a week-end, you will nearby hotels or motels to accommodate your needs. If you are into shopping, you will find reasonably priced boutiques and shops to go on a spree. It's my observation that to truly enjoy the beach, you have to spend more than 1 day there. Let the kids go loose on the sand. While you find a nice spot to sit down by the feet of the pier, you will watch the kids building castles in the sand. Depending on the time of your visit, the wind may cause a sand storm that throws sand up the stairs leading to the shore lines. Just like some of my colleagues did last time, you just have to turn your back and get down. All I did was to just run down in a few seconds.

Are you a bird watcher?

The seagulls and other types of sea birds are ever present. They appear to be very tamed. Some people even feed them. Others try to stay away from the excrement-dropping seagulls in flight. I have never seen anybody getting pooped on. By the time they are ready to leave the beach, they may get pooped up, exhausted by all the activities on the sand. Being a huge frisbee thrower, I will invite you to buy a couple of them. If you don't have somebody to throw them to, just throw them out and attempt to catch them. By the time you stop this game, you will be surprised by overall workout you will have. Running in the sand helps you build stamina. No matter what, Pismo is a very popular destination for bird watchers. They come from all over the world to enjoy their time on this vast expanse of beach areas. In the background up in the hill, you will see all the new, expensive real estate. Right on the beach, you can see some parents playing with their kids in the dunes.

Visitors to the Pismo State Beach also come to get a chance to see the annual Winter migration of monarch butterflies. They arrive by thousands in their haven by the sea. While I was there, I overhead two ladies speaking French. So I responded and greeted them. They were from Belgium. They were vacationing at Pismo because of the beach, the butterflies and the overall amenities.

Other activities you can take part in

If you are into hiking, you can do so right on the sand. If you are interested in surf fishing and digging for the famous Pismo clam, you will have ample opportunities to engage into your hobby.

Are your kids into kite-flying?

Kite-flying is not only for kids. It's also for adults. I have a few kites. Any way, if you are wondering about kite shops, you will find a few of them over there. There are all kinds of kites you can purchase. It all depends on your taste. While I was there, the wind was too strong to fly a kite. So I had to leave my butterfly kite in the trunk of my car.

How about the food? Tell me about the restaurants
Leave your crab at the beach

If you are on the beach, you want to eat seafood. My colleagues and I wanted to go to the famous Mclintocks, but it was closed by the time we get there. If only we knew that they follow a strict schedule during the week days, we would have gone earlier and shopped afterwards. At any rate, we decided to find a different spot. We found it in **www.crackedcrab.com.** We had a blast. From a big bucket for two to local king salmon, live local rock crab dinner, crab cakes, grilled oysters and fish and chips, you can't go wrong there. The atmosphere at the restaurant is pretty nice for that early afternoon. I can imagine what it is like in the evening when all the young people, business people start coming in for dinners or when a band decides to play in the background.

How To Reach Cracked Crab?

FROM THE NORTH (San Luis Obispo, Paso Robles, Atascadero, San Francisco, etc) US 101 south to the "Pismo Beach / South 1" exit. At the stop sign turn left (Price Street). They are six or seven very short blocks down on the right, just before the Landmark Hotel.

FROM THE SOUTH (Arroyo Grande, Santa Maria, Santa Barbara, Ventura, L.A., Etc) US 101 north to the "Price Street, Downtown Pismo Beach" exit. Keep going forward three or four very short blocks. They are on the left, just past the Landmark Hotel.

Bear in mind that this is just a sample of the great restaurants you can eat at. Enjoy your time if you have a chance to make it to Pismo State Beach.

Is it a recommendation?
Yes, definitely. It's a family-friendly beach. I hope that you are going to have fun there.

Sacramento, the State Capital of California

Pros
Spring is the best time to visit; A city with charms.

Cons
Heat can be numbing

The Bottom Line
As the capital of California, Sacramento may be your destination for many reasons. If you are there for a short time, you need to know where to have fun.

I have been to many state capitals and many cities of various countries, but after visiting Sacramento, I will admit that I fall for its charms. They are unique. Standing from the steps of the State Capitol, you can see all the way down to the Sacramento bridge. Your first order of business will be to visit the Capitol. Once you start climbing the steps at the west entrance, you will see the massive bronze State Seal which measures 10 feet. It was made by inmates from San Quentin Prison. While I was there, I observed a lot of people using this area for political speeches, a Grassroots rally (in support with the handicapped and developmentally disabled). Various people spoke about the issues faced by this population, issues such as a good salary for those who are working with them and lack of housing for the consumers etc. Promises were made by the leaders.

Access to the public: Offices appear accessible

One of the things that struck my group was the apparent accessibility of the public servants' offices. They are located on the first floor. This is unlike many other places where such offices would be located at the nth floor. Able-bodied taxpayer as well as disabled could easily tour these offices. As soon as you enter the building, you will get to the display of various counties of the State. Look up and explore the Rotunda. Various historic museums are located on the first floor. Don't hesitate to ask a guide to give you a tour. Guides are stationed there. From the rotunda, you will reflect at the majestic beauty, splendor and richness of the State of California. It is truly a great building that most Californian tax-payers can be proud of. You can imagine the indignity of such vandalism act by an angry driver who smashed his big rig onto the pillars of the Capitol. Reparations are under way and will cost close to $5000,000! *Find out whether you are fit or not:* Take the stairs to the sixth floor instead of taking the elevators which are fast, but can be busy. Get your daily exercise done there!

Landscape and surrounding architecture

I remain impressed by the amount of shade trees that exist around the Capitol building. It is said that many of these large trees are part of the original planting of 1870 that go from L to N and 10th to 12th streets. Some of the trees are Deodar cedars, Italian stone pines, tulip trees, southern magnolias, redwoods and cypress trees. As you walk around the building, you can run into Atlas cedars, pepper trees, Mexican and California fan palms. I start to think that my decision to love the city may stem from the existence of all the trees the city has.

Old Sacramento: A great visit on boardwalks and amidst horse-drawn carriages

I don't want to go as far as comparing Sacramento to New Orleans. But, some of the features of Old Sacramento may lead somebody to think this way. The sheer amount of shops and horse-drawn carriages and the number of people are some of the common features. My favorite hanging-out area is to have lunch at the Fat City Café and Bar. I also like going to spend some time in front of the Delta King Hotels on the boards facing the Sacramento River. With the ice cream shop just a few steps away, on a good Spring evening, this can be a nice place to enjoy the weather. Old Sacramento has all the great restaurants, clubs, bars and clubs to have a good time. I remember entering a kite store where the average kite costs $30.00 and up to $400 and plus.

If you visit Old Sacramento, don't forget to the California State Railroad Museum. Go to the Laughs Unlimited Comedy Club at the end of Front Street close to the wide variety of shops. Street parking is OK. If you can't find one, head to the nearby paid garages. Depending on when you go there, it can be hot, but you will have a good time. Summer is usually hot, but if you go there in the Spring, you will be just fine.

Santa Monica: The Liveliest City on Highway 1:

Spring Break Destination Mecca

Pro: Lots to do and see; great eateries for foodies; exercises, outdoors chess;

If you want to see people and get seen, you need to go to Santa Monica. Lots of sea, sand, sun and fun to have!

You may have been missing out on a great California beach town to spend your holiday in if you don't read this review. The following one is the result of my recent trip to this quaint and lively city by the sea. Santa Monica, located at the western end of famed Route 66 and the crossroads of the Pacific Coast Highway and the Santa Monica Freeway which is Interstate 10, was the playground of my family during our Fall travels to the coast. If we adults had fun, our kids had a ball. What's clear is that despite the fact Santa Monica is a stars' playground, it is very appealing and attractive to kids. Everything is right there and very accessible.

How did we end up picking this city?

After our trip to Huntington Beach for our daughter's Cheerleading competition, we decided that we would have a break. So we looked at our work schedule and decided to use some of our vacation time. Never have we missed the opportunity to travel in the Fall. It's the best of the year to travel with kids in tow. Beach destinations are never too crowded. You have the feeling that you have the whole place to yourself and kids. We knew it would not be the same in Santa Monica. Before settling down, my friends and I considered the city as our stumping grounds. After a hard week of classroom and projects, the way we rewarded our efforts was to head to the beach. So way before the kids came, we knew our way around the city. Now with kids, we would not be able to stay up all night and sleep just a few hours before hitting the next club.

How to reach Santa Monica and what to expect there?

Location: Santa Monica is about 8 miles from Los Angeles International Airport and 13 miles from downtown L.A. It's located right on the famous Highway 1 traveled by most stars from Hollywood on their way to this fun city. Does the well-known $1 billion Getty Center ring a bell? Well, this museum is located right the hills of Santa Monica. Now you start seeing why you should visit Santa Monica. How about Baywatch with Pamela Anderson and David Hasseldorf? Santa Monica is the place where most of the series was filmed before its last location in Hawaii. You may have heard about the classic, historic "Muscle Beach" guys? Do the following names ring a bell in the world of fitness? Jack Lalanne and Joe Gold are some of the names you may remember from that great of guys who inspired others with their physical prowess.

Forget about everything else, let's see how my kids and I had fun

Day 1: *Visit to the Santa Monica Pier*

With our kids, we had to find the kids' stuff first. Before heading to the nearby rides, we had a pleasant surprise from a street performer who has never ceased to delight tourists and families alike. Mr. "Bubble Man" was providing lots of fun to everybody on the pier. My son spotted him first and started running toward his location. Kids and adults were chasing huge bubbles. He was never tired of blowing them to please his audience. To tell you the truth, I was surprised to have seen him still on the pier. For some time, there had been some push from the city council and others to get him off the pier. It appears that he survived these personal attacks. When his fans rose to defend him, these people appeared to give in. What can a man who is blowing bubbles for kids and tourists do to harm the image of the city? In fact, he appears to add to or enhance it. How many cities have unselfish people like the bubble man? Only Berkeley had the late Charles as the famous "Smile and Greeting guy!"

Distractions abound on the pier. You will see musicians trying to get the passersby's attention. They play a large variety of instruments. They are groups and solo presentations. They play for whomever cares about listening. Depending on your generosity, you may want to reward their efforts by tipping them. I did not see any of them pushing their hats in any tourists' face.

Any vacationers in Santa Monica will find something they can appreciate. Whether you are interested in great foods, you will fall in love with the large variety of culinary styles existing in this beach town. I will warn you that some of them may be very exotic. The taste may be different, but you will not forget the names of restaurants such as Typhoon, Michael's and Chinois where you will be served French, Chinese and Asian-based haute cuisine. Whereas I enjoyed my time and the foods served by Chinois, my wife fell for Michael's and its decor. In fact, I will have to agree with her on the way we felt once we were dining. The atmosphere is very awe-inspiring and soothing. Maybe it was so after spending so much time in the sun, on the beach, playing around with the kids building sand castles.

Toward the end of the day, we took our spots on the beach to throw frisbees and watch some hard and lean bodies play volleyball. The waves were not scary. They were very gentle. We watched our kids running away from them as if they wanted to race them to the shores. Needless to say that there were no surfers to intrude on the various nearby sunbathers! There's no wave. It's not like Huntington Beach and other beach fronts. Most likely, those who want to surf go out to Malibu on the North. Keep in mind that Redondo beach is also a great place to be. Tourists and locals flock to both of these places.

Day 2:

I got early and slipped into my workout wear. Armed with my cell phones, I headed out after living my wife a note. I did not want to wake her up because we stayed up late the night before. The kids were still asleep. I wanted to check out the morning hours at Santa Monica. Staying right on the beach helps you take part in this classic routine. We stayed at Hotel Oceana which overlooks the Pacific on Ocean Avenue. By the way, if you want find other venues. You can stay at Shutters on the Beach, Casa del Mara and Viceroy.

I immediately joined the rest of the early birds. Being in Santa Monica helps you fit in easily. It's time to adopt a healthy attitude. With its miles of paths for walking, jogging, cycling and skating, this city with the fittest residents in California. I was surprised to find people playing chess at the well-known Chess park which is close to the original Muscle Beach. It reportedly can accommodate up to 80 players. World-class and amateurs try to develop their skills right there. The Chess board is built on the sand with large chess pieces. After jogging for about 2 hours, I returned to the hotel to take a shower and eat breakfast. The kids were already up and ready to head out.

By 10 am, my family and I went to the Third Street Promenade. People started arriving by busloads. Fortunately, this is a car-free shopping, dining and fun-filled area. I wanted my wife and daughter to dance to Salsa. It's not unusual to find large groups of people dancing in the streets. Whatever musical style you have heard about, you will find samples of it being played and danced to at the Third Street Promenade. The atmosphere here reminds me of Calle Ocho in Miami, Florida where you can listen to all kinds of Cuban Salsa and son blaring from speakers in nearby stores and restaurants. It's like life lived in the open! It's a true party every day.

Santa Monica is kids and tourists-friendly

There is no doubt that this city takes great pride in its image. Just contact the Santa Monica Visitor Center and you will soon realize how important it is to the city. If you ask any local and tourist, they will tell you that the heart of the city resides in the pier. That's where actions happen. It boasts very creative shops, boutiques, rides on the world's first solar-powered Ferris wheel, night clubs such as the Sand & Sea club and many others. Of all the attractions, the 3 ½ miles of honey-colored sand remains my kids' favorite. As for me, there is no better feeling than having your face being caressed by cool breeze while sitting in the low tides playing dominos. No it's not a fantasy.

Anybody can visit Santa Monica to have a fun time.

Good travel. Hope to run into you there some time soon.

Temporary Troubles, Eternal Glory

Christmas time is the time to be together with loved ones and with those who matter to us a lot. This year's Christmas season will be more meaningful for many of us in this country and around the world. It's a time when we can truly count our blessings in light of all the conflicts, acts of violence, war, diseases, the terrorist spread of anthrax in our mail system, talks of WMD and bioterrorism.

The tragedy of Sept. 11 is still fresh on our collective minds. There is no way we will forget those who laid their lives at the great altar of service. The first celebration of Christmas after those horrible acts finds us more meditative and mindful of our position in the larger community. Many other Christmas celebrations will follow in the years ahead. We are the keepers of our brothers and sisters. We become more united than ever before despite all the things that existed out there to divide us. The enemies might have tried to divide us, but we did not get into their traps. We stood tall and united in the midst of our calamities and tribulations.

The temporary troubles of our lives are nothing in comparison with the eternal glory we are called to have in the Father of all comfort (2 Corinthians 2:3-4). In these days of tremendous pain, it is good to go back to the things that bring us comfort, the things we are familiar with. Family, friendship, religion, strong sense of community, flag, storytelling and patriotism are all the things that become important in our lives since Sept. 11. This is why our officials encouraged us to go back to our normal routine despite all the changes that suddenly became part of our world. Our world changed on 9-11. Now we can talk about pre-911 and post-911. They will be for ever known as historical markers or landmarks.

No matter how much change we have lately witnessed, we want to stick to the constant points of our life. There is no doubt that we were truly shaken by the anthrax scare. We knew that we had to be careful with something that has become part of our lives. For far too long, we have taken our snail mail for granted. When we saw that our mail men and women start becoming victims of the terrorist acts, we knew that those changes would affect us personally. This is why we need to be more appreciative and thankful for these people in our lives. How many times have we taken the time to purposefully say a few words of thanks to these brave men and women who deliver our mail to us in good and bad times? How many times have we personally thanked our dry cleaner workers? How about the men in uniform, the firefighters, rescue workers, police officers, emergency medical workers and even the rescue dogs? It makes sense that these people did not think twice to rush to the burning towers to help, guide, comfort others who were facing certain death? They rushed in to humanize and diminish the suffering of complete strangers. They REACHED out to them. They did something to alleviate their excruciating pain. As a grateful society, we respond by recognizing their heroic acts. In a matter of minutes, days and months, they have reclaimed the title that surely belongs to them.

These ordinary men and women did not become our heroes because of their excellent beauty (even though most of them are beautiful), they became our heroes for their unselfish, altruistic acts on behalf of thousands. Even on earth, their recognition and rewards are greater than most others.

From the smoldering rubbles rose goodness. It's true that the hearts of many people in this country and all over the world ache, they have become witnesses of history. It has been history in the making ever since these tragic, horrific days befell our country. Goodness surely germinated and rose from the ruins of such major losses of lives and property. Grief took over our mind. The level of atrocity is unimaginable. Men have become their own fiercest enemies. They are bent on destroying themselves for each time a man dies, a part of another man also dies. If anything, the heinous acts of Sept. 11 make us realize the value of being connected to our community and the value of interdependence.

All over the world, prayer vigils were held. Churches saw an upsurge in attendance. Neighbors who never said hi to each other finally realized that they had so much to share. They are talking. Even major cities' crime rates decline for the few days after the tragedy. Once for all, people matter. Relationships matter. It's ok to grieve. It's ok to look for public comfort and inspirational or spiritual matters. The stock market becomes less relevant. Our materialistic ambitions are set aside for a while. Our selfish ways become the antithesis to this kind of 1-for-all sense of community.

Compassion becomes more than a simple word. Seize the day. Live today and forget the past and even the future. How many of us wouldn't like to sustain this kind of spirit of America at its best? Even on busy streets, complete strangers take time to say hi. They don't seem to be peering down your throats without even nodding your way or recognizing you are around. Our hearts become open to the needs of our neighbors. That's how it should have been all along! We may have finally realized that we are all on the same boat of life.

Life is too short for us to waste it. Let's use it to contribute to our world and matter to others. Our life is like a flower. Job 14:2. No matter what may have come our way, we know that victory, glory awaits in the near future. 2 Corinthians 4:1, 7-8, 17-18;

Please meditate over this passage: "God is our refuge and strength, a very present help in trouble. Therefore we will not fear, even though the earth be removed, and though the mountains be carried into the midst of the sea.." Psalm 46: 1-2.

Let's sustain the spirit of America at its best! We are a nation of strong faith, conviction and determination

The American Good Life

It's all about a state of mind backed by the $ sign and investments
Being able to shop at a sophisticated boutique defines it for some
For others, it's being able to do as they see fit
How about owning a beautiful home in the suburbs?
Owning real estate in San Francisco, Southern California or
anywhere else places you closer to that unique feeling
Is it being able to go from one golf course to the next
with the best equipment that money can buy?
Is it a good job? How about a career?
It must powerful friends in high places
Donald Trump has all these material things that a person can want
Bill and Melinda Gates sit on top of a large fortune at Microsoft
Mr. Buffet is among the richest Americans of our times
Everybody wants the good life that is reduced to consumerism
It's as evident as a muscled car, a tall truck whose wheels
and frame perch the young drivers who need wisdom
For the farmer, rancher and fruit grower, the good life starts
with the knowledge that his land, crops, cattle are safe
No cattle and crop thefts. No foreclosure. No low prices
for products that required initial investments and ongoing payments
Is it a cabin in the woods? How about a second home in the foothills?
Who is enjoying the good life? When is it attained? Can one know it?
The snow that collects in the Sierra is the source of many good things
There will be enough water to use and irrigate the fertile fields of the Valley
Because without it, the San Joaquin Valley returns to her forbidden desert status
Returning from back-breaking work in the fields, the laborer has a bowl of chili
Wait a minute! He has more to be thankful for: health, job and family
"People do not live by bread alone. They often need beauty, creativity and buttering up."
He can afford to buy a cake for his daughter's birthday. He provides for her
His wife is also a woman in agriculture. She creates magic every day at home
Without the grower, rancher, farmworker or farmer's wife, California can't retain
her #1 position in agriculture. Such women have been around for ever!
Long live cowgirls, the true stewards of the land!
They once tamed the Wild West. They conquered it with their sweat and sighs
Not known to take a break from the intensity of farm labor, they march on

Therefore, the good life comes to symbolize hard work from all
No pain, no gain! The good life is a moving target.
Is it Yoga? Membership to an exclusive club?
Is it the enjoyment of one's civil rights?
Meditation and prayers often soften the blows of life.
There is no good life without great balance and self-control
Being able to be an integral part of the modern economy adds a certain level
of connection, inclusiveness, and membership into a greater body

The Migration to the North

They left the South in the middle of the night
They turned their back on the cotton fields,
tradition and everything else they knew
No longer was life worth living on the large plantations
where the legacy of slavery and Jim Crow suffocated them
They bid farewell to all the past symbols and history
Some could not take the burden any longer in the '30s, '40s
Others were fed up with the blowing dirt
and soot that infiltrated and permeated everything
They became the casualties of the Dust Bowl era
In droves, they came to northern cities leaving behind
their farms, dying animals and barn. They were attracted
by the promises of a new life, job, and education
Chicago, Detroit, Oklahoma, California beckoned them
Long and crowded bus and train rides took them to the new frontier
A new beginning awaited them in the West's industrial centers
From sharecroppers to wage earners, from rural dwellers to
city residents, those new migrants accepted the challenge
of life in a strange land with many weather patterns
From field workers to land owners, they planted roots
The Harlem Renaissance got stretched to the West Coast
Black and White migrants' skills became wanted
in San Francisco, San Diego, Oakland and other areas
There were lots of jobs to be had up and down
the huge fertile farmlands of the Central Valley
Over time, with the sweat of their forehead,
their living conditions got improved. Prosperity and thrift
eventually led them to the sacred temple of consumer culture
Things such as consumption, leisure, and material abundance,
 department stores, advertising, mass-produced cars, and suburbs
transformed the American economy, society and politics.

Clovis, California

She has a vibrant downtown where people walk, shop,
browse storefronts, chat and drink designer coffee
On your way to Squaw Valley, Yosemite and Kings Canyon,
stop by to get acquainted with her residents and antique shops,
bookshops and specialized, quaint boutiques
Clovis is an idyllic town nestled in the heart of the Central Valley
She is blessed by nature and geography, rustic view
pastoral fields, orchards and groves
She lies at the gates of the foothills
What are her main attractions? Did you say her residents and tourism are?
They must be her old brown street signs, brick homes, and store porches
How about the perceived and real high quality of life?
Some say the comparatively low crime rate is her main attraction
Others enjoy the ego boost and status of a Clovis address
For them, that's the end of real estate discrimination
Why do family home buyers prefer her real estate?
Why do they go to great lengths to be part of her city life?
Is it the Big hat festival's joie de vivre? Or is the rodeo with all
her bedecked corrals, elegant cowboys and cowgirls?
Is it the Strawberry festival in May? Is it the pole vault competition?
Or is it the product of her leaders' vision and planning?
It must be a Clovis attitude, a Clovis thing!
Planning and order are valued over here
Whatever you say it is, it's been working well for a long time now
More and more out-of-towners want to flock to her boundaries
Some claim that they want their kids to go to Clovis schools
They are willing to pay a premium to give them a head start
Test scores, school ratings, accessibility, and services drive their decisions
So do location, property values and good neighborhood schools
A few checks of the California Department of Education web site
www.cde.ca.gov convince many new residents to brave the heat of the valley
Educated parents who care about the Academic Performance Index (API)
swell the ranks of those who want to outbid each other as new lots get available
The tractor operator knows very well the story of these new tracks
He has been clearing the fields of peach, plum, almond, nectarine and orange trees
He hikes his price many times as more and more developers want his service
His tractor breaks down the old canals that once irrigated and crisscrossed the land
A heavy machine operator is a very practical man. He knows very well
that these acres that grew our celebrated fruits and nuts are gone for ever
He also knows that people need homes to raise their families.
Their kids need a good quality of education made available by the CUSD
From the high seat of his bulldozer, he meters out advice to whoever wants to listen
As he eats his lunch, between bites, he lifts up his head to gaze upon the nearby bloom,

He quickly realizes that his once small city has become a top relocation magnet
A Brand New Day In San Francisco

Quite new to some, in fact, new to many of us
but never a nuisance to others whose fight
for recognition, equality and a piece of paper
has been ongoing in our great democracy
A powerful minority defined by their sexual orientation
wants to have their voice heard in the political landscape
Something to get used to or something whose time
may have come just like many other things have in this country
Indeed, quite a bold move by anyone on Valentine's Day
The celebration of same-sex marriages hits Sacramento as a storm
Men embracing men, women holding hands with women
leap at the chance to wed or tie the knots just like
a man and a woman often do on the steps of the state capitol
or elsewhere on any Valentine's Day

Wedding parties, bells, choruses, cheers and wishes of health and prosperity
abound in this city by the bay. Out-of-town couples continue to arrive
Believing in the principles that all people are created equal
"I pronounce you man and man or woman and woman," said the recorder
"Go your way. Live in sin no more." With their marriage licence in hand,
The young biracial couple smiled, kissed each other and exited the platform
How compelling is the need to do the right thing in God's eyes?
That very minute, the walls of more than 6,000 years of tradition
have fallen like water rushing down the corrals of an old dam
Gays, lesbians, metrosexuals and all other alternative groups
braved the natural elements to reach their goals
Love conjures sacrifices they're willing to subject themselves to
"African-Americans and other minority groups suffered for their civil rights,"
said a young couple to an opponent of the same-sex marriage.
"You are the dregs of society. Read the Bible," called out an opposing group
"Neither the distractions by heterosexual onlookers nor the threats
of reversing our new right and opportunity to wed will keep us away," they replied.

San Francisco's historic move galvanized many gay and lesbian couples
around the nation. New Mexico and New York jumped on the bandwagon
They give more than a civil union; they are allowing the real thing, marriage
From Vermont to San Francisco, a loud message is going out to heterosexuals
who don't take their vows seriously
Wake up now and stop the high incidence of divorces and headache
You have something that others have been deprived from for far too long
They covet your privileges and want the same rights you have.
Politicians from all parties will continue to debate these issues for a long time
Gay and lesbian couples will show their financial muscles and organization skills

A new thing has indeed hit San Francisco. As a whole, society has to define
what's normal and abnormal, what's natural and unnatural once more
Gays and lesbians are our neighbors who also need to be validated
They want love and recognition as they make contributions to societies
Who will cast the first stone? And Jesus took time for the ostracized harlot.

Water and the Blossom

Enjoy the view of the blossom while it lasts
Take in everything nature has to offer
The blooms will soon fall down
Fruits and nuts will appear on the trees
Without rain and pumped water,
there won't be any of these seasonal wonders
California's farms as well as towns are competing
for the same precious resource, the new gold of developments
Let the water flow to east-side farms where juicy peaches,
nectarines, plums, pears and apples are grown
Let it flow to the Westside where melons and almonds are grown
Let there be enough water to quench the thirst of our cities too!
May local farmers, growers and ranchers continue to make a living
out of farming and operating their ranch to keep their water shares around!
Dreadful will be the day when this precious liquid has to be sold to
far-flung cities where flowers instead of deciduous fruits will be harvested
May water speculators and brokers stay away from the water districts that
manage our water distribution through elaborate waterways, ditches and canals!
We don't want to see a repeat of the Owens Valley in the Central Valley
Trees need water to grow in this desert. A dust bowl is to be avoided at all costs
Take the water away and the land will be lonely
Blooming orchards and groves will disappear. Our belly will rely on exports
There is greater safety in home-grown or locally grown foods, fruits and nuts
For a country that can't feed itself tends to lose its defense little by little
Let there be enough water for the cotton and alfalfa fields of Mendota and Firebaugh
Let there be enough water of the San Joaquin and Kings Rivers
to irrigate the corn fields near the dairy farms of Chowchilla and Tulare

Blooming Orchards

Driving in the rural areas of California
On a stormy day
The rain drops are pelting the blooms
On the almond, peach, nectarine and plum trees
Honeybees don't leave their hives to seek nectar
Weather conditions have been confusing them
A bright warm day is often succeeded by many rainy ones
Hanford and Kerman almond growers would like it
Otherwise,
But nobody can time Mother Nature
There's a time for everything under the sun
There's a time to bloom; there is a time to bear fruits
If the bees don't fend out to pollinate, the yields will be small

This is the time to open oneself to the view of the back country
This is also the time to watch the deep green grass on the rangeland
One can't help but appreciating the vanishing lines and silhouettes
Of cattle grazing on huge acres of open fields
Alone on the roads
but always surrounded by blooming fields on one side
and wind-whipped tumbleweeds that get stopped by fences on the other side
Huge gray clouds can be spotted on top of the trees
With the snow-capped Sierra Nevada in the background
Long live open roads, sky and fields!

Harvest Ladder

It's harvest season again all over the Valley
Men and women are moving heavy agriculture ladders
and crates laden with beautiful and juicy fruits
to the end of the fields where the loading station is
How delectable and succulent are these peaches, nectarines and plums?
Perspiration soaks the pickers' shirts from early morning to noon
Some workers are thinking about the cool Spring and Fall days
Others are escaping to the coast's daily mist and occasional fog
Valley residents have been fleeing the heat of these fertile fields
From the native residents in times past to the current Valley dwellers
Who would not like to escape to the soothing, cooling coastal towns
and river bluffs under such working conditions?
A clear misery for the men and women but a boon
and a great thing for all the growers and their fruits
Harvest time is not supposed to be the season of rain
The consuming heat must speed the ripening process
Those overcome by the hot sun seek refuge under
the shade of these beautiful and overloaded deciduous trees
Moving about the land becomes a necessary chore
Only riding along the fruit trail in the comfort of one's car is easier
No more worry about keeping the production quota for the day!
Foreman and fellow crew members share their survival techniques
Once the fruit harvest is over, owners and workers will be able
to spend one or two week-ends cooling down on the beach
Morro Bay, Pismo, Carpentier and Santa Barbara beaches beckon
It's time for them to rejoice, ride three wheelers around the Oceano shores
It's time to eat crabs, lobsters, fresh fish, tell stories late at night
by the bonfire and under thick blankets in the back of their vehicles
It's also time to swim, loathe, bathe and lazily lay down, ride motor bikes
It's time to make the annual pilgrimage to Hearst Castle, Cambria,
posh boutiques and art galleries strategically located all along the coastal range
The memory of the stuck fishing rod will not be forgotten soon
The families will return home with enough stories of great catch to tell
They'll be busy around the farm as always. They'll wait for the next season.

Golden Vineyards

Welcome to Napa, Sonoma and Mendocino
Welcome to the land of the superb vines and wine
Why not Modesto, Visalia, Selma, and Fresno?
Tasting signs are everywhere to enjoy
once you cross the new frontier and the city's boundaries
Against the background of this bright blue sky
with rolling white clouds, a picture-perfect romance is set
Temples are built to champion wineries with superstar wines
Altars are erected to worship the best wine products that
have ever touched our palate. A sip here and a full glass over there
Vintners, winemakers and viticulturists have grown their vines
from their own r&d labs and the best European stocks
It's a mixture of the best that Italy, Germany, Spain, France
can give to the new world and specially the West Coast
Napa, Sonoma and Mendocino are the meccas
of the California's booming wine industry
From the mission San Francisco solano de Sonoma, former priests,
Buena Vista's early wine experience with shade oaks and eucalyptus,
Charles Krug Wineries, Robert Mondavi Winery, Coppola Winery
to the wineries located between Santa Barbara and Cambria,
any wine connoisseur and tourist can find the exact match for their taste
Gaze upon the green rolling hills dotted
with oaks and wind-breaking trees.
Take a look at the cover crops between the parallel rows of vines
Look beyond the winery mansion on top of the hill
and recognize once for all the sustainability and suitability
of this precious land. Men become the stewards of nature
Vineyards and wineries show the continuity and vision of the forebears
New immigrants follow in the well-disced rows and footsteps
of older ones among these vines and open riches
The new economy resides in the land among these grapes and raisins
Modesto, Madera, Fresno and California State University Fresno or
Fresno State wines are leaving their own imprints
on the consumer's taste buds
Long live California wine country!

Sanger, CA

Sanger comes alive with fragrance and color
this time of the year, at Blossom Trail Fest
Between the end of February and early March,
it's the place to be. It's also the place to see bees
Every year, this blessed corner of the huge California's
agricultural empire offers a prized decor to tourists
Almond, peach, plum, nectarine trees are now in full bloom
Their white, pink and purple petals are falling
They form a huge snow-like carpet around the tree trunks
All along the Blossom trail,
beehives are stacked on top of each other
Unlike the previous cold and rainy days, bees are abuzz today
They like the above 55-degree temperature
Water from nearby pumps and the river continues to irrigate
New green leaves will hide the new fruits
For sure, the trees have been pollinated
To assure greater yields, a mid-season pruning will take place
Fruit lovers will soon stop by the roadside fruit stands
to enjoy the juicy early-season strawberries
We'll have them around all the way to the harvest of
plums, apricots, peaches, nectarines in May, June, July and August
The Blossom Trail will be succeeded by the Fruit Trail
in an ever-ending succession of blooms and harvest
Co-existence is the way of the future
New track or housing trail will soon be created
Never will the San Joaquin Valley become Los Angeles
Let the Orange Trail continue to attract visitors to the Valley!
Delve into the landscape and lore of the Fresno-Clovis areas
Plunge into the history of Sanger, Reedley, Fowler and Selma
Welcome to the land of exceptional beauty
where men, God, topography and nature create harmony
May this co-existence lead to sustainability and last for ever!

The Vast Wilderness

Sustainability and protection must be intertwined
Protect wild areas for future generations

Keep them accessible to the public
Don't let them become private properties

as exemplified by the cases of limited or no
access to beaches locked behind huge walls

Those with more power, money and connection
dictate the new rules of coastal living and access

Our grandchildren will appreciate our efforts
on their behalf. Protect our resources and

be good stewards to the environment
You and I have long taken it for granted

Celebrate the 1964 wilderness act
which makes large expanse of California
accessible to all Californians and tourists
Let's all enjoy our forests, dunes, beaches and deserts

Convivialis: Food and Romance

The romance of good foods should be
the fuel of any lasting and meaningful relationships

sensual foods add spice to our love live
call them chocolate, oysters, figs, conch, lobster

peach, mango, strawberries, cherries, caviar etc
ordinary foods grown with love and

shopped with care and planning become great meals
only two lovers can experience the thrill

of cooking together under the same roof
for her, cooking and baking are a celebration of

her love and devotion to the family
good food is good romance

good romance is also nurturing
while writing, doing yoga, working, exercising and

meditating may be calming
cooking and dealing with cookware and burners

are her healing respite. They are the spouse's expression
of intimacy. The taste buds are already turned on before

the plates reach the table on this special occasion
a nectarine, plum, avocado, and watermelon slice add

to the list of aphrodisiac foods we've all come to appreciate
how about some great pasta, raspberry, carrot cake and

favorite ice cream consumed at candlelight in the Summer night?
there's no more need to hurry. Take small bites among whispers

great victuals and conviviality create the right atmosphere
there's no need to overeat because many good days are ahead

Chili On Top Of Hot Dogs

Give me life; give me chile
Is it California Chile, Texas Chili or the New Mexico type?

Yes, chili made from huge chunks of ground meat
with beans or frijoles and lots of tomato

Give me a hot and inspiring taste of chili
that is served with grated cheese, sour cream, chopped onions

Please add to my serving some oyster crackers, Saltines
cornbread, and spaghetti. This is a stew made for westerners

on black cast-iron pots passed from one generation of cowboys
to the next one. Chile peppers grown from the fields of the Valley

and all over the western territories become a hit culinary addition
Enjoy a serving of chili verde, add a concoction of fresh chiles

to your palate -Not the ground dried chiles that lead to chili powder
Expose your freshly picked chiles to the baking California sun

and observe their leathery and twisted colorful beauty
Find chili powder at the local ethnic tiendas, mercados

and the regular supermarket shelves of your city
From Florida to California, from Maine to New York

Treat your palate with a few servings of black bean chili, white chili,
seafood chili loaded with clams, lobster, shrimp, sea scallops, and salmon

Feel free to make up your own stew, prepare your own chili
Lots of improvisations with Chili peppers. Long live chile con carne!

Fallen Angels

Shocked and furious, the community rode down to leave teddy bears,
flowers, stuffed animals, music sheets and poems at the makeshift memorial

Marcus adopted the lifestyle of the current times
Before the killings, he was an alleged real estate man

who buys and sells houses. He must have squeezed some capital
He also wrote "big books" probably about his long descent into darkness

and repaired his chrome-laden yellow bus late at night with his women
10 ornate caskets filled the converted office's living room

while 9 bodies of his own children were stacked in a back bedroom
Neighbors are now saying that he liked to barbecue foul meat when

he was not making noise building a spa on the bus
With his boat anchored on the coast, he flees the valley's heat

just like he has managed to evade the radar of public agencies,
child protective services, local authorities and schools

Was it a ritual killing? a cult? Why would a man kill all these people?
Was it the last blow in a long trajectory of flight from real life?

How long has he been subjugating his own kids to these abuses?
Is the murder the peak or evolution of his threats and exploitation?

Marcus' unkempt profile finally revealed the depth of his depravity
His world was one of abuse, servile exploitation, disrespect, incest,

threats and murder. He was too far down to give a chance
to his own kids, his own blood. Too late for anybody to jump to their rescue!

The police chief, onlookers and the mayor fought back tears while
the police officers and SWAT Team were placed on administrative leave

Carved in Malaysia, the 10 coffins were taken away
as evidence. His pride and joy, the old school bus, was moved

From the battlefield of their own home, their bodies were retrieved
Standing as one, the community buried her dead sons and daughters

Prophecy and Revelations

Farewell to the Blossom Trail
Farewell to the San Joaquin Valley's fertile fields
where our kids play in the polluted air that
makes them sick of asthma most days of the year
The raisin and stone fruit farmers are bidding adieu
to the land they've known all their lives
They've seen their water diverted to urban areas
where new housing tracts are always on track
Los Angeles' orange fields are long gone
The barren hillsides see a burst of new building activities
Farewell to the roadside strawberry, melon, apple,
nectarine, peach, orange and grape stands
There won't be any more use of methyl bromide
to kill insects, weeds and control plantations
There won't be any more traditions to hold on to
No more attachments to the fatherland!
No more talk about streams and salmon run!
Quality of life crimes, poverty and joblessness
will become unbearable when the Valley
loses its traditional identity
How about moving to a new subdivision in Southern Calif.?
The former Valley residents can't afford to live there either
They become lost upon the surface of the golden state
 The liquid gold has long been taken away
Southern California will no longer have the fresh foods,
fruits and vegetables of the Valley.
Our stomach will depend on China, Chile and Mexico more
For the seeds have no more water to germinate
Farewell to the madness and greed that make us lose the treasure!
Farewell to the Blossom Trail, Fruit Trail and Orange Blossom Trail

2008 Spring Break

Postcard from Pismo Beach, Calif.

The beach is crowded with students and bikers. Oceano Dunes at Pismo is seeing heavy traffic. The main road running right in front of the Cracked Crab in downtown Pismo is renovated. Large bouquets of flowers enhance the dividers and islands. Massive CHP and Police presence is necessary in front of the Billiards and Flash Cafe. They have to direct foot traffic and regular traffic. These two places serve respectively the best fish and chips and clam chowder. Chele's restaurant makes a killing. We want to have dinner at the Cracked Crab. We only drive right by it. There is no way we will find an available parking space. Besides, it is not conducive to having children around. The bikers have the best of anybody there. You know, they have a little too much fun.

The weather is gorgeous. I think it's kind of cold. Don't say this to Caleb who wants to be a surfer. He watched a lot of cartoons with surfing dudes. We buy him a board. He wants a wet suit. We only buy him a body warmer and short. See his picture. He gets scared by the crashing waves and can't catch a wave at all. Cassandra and I caught a few big ones. As for Cassandra, she is having a blast with one of her classmates whose parents happen to be on the same beach. She gets to spend an hour playing with her on the other side of the dunes. Colby is enjoying the ocean for the first time. Katrina enjoys every minute of it except for some beach bugs to which she appears to be allergic.

All in all, it's a great time to travel with little ones.

The Haitan Granmother
By Joseph J. Charles

Dizzy and covered with dirt and sweat,
The Haitian grandmother does not give up
Au contraire, she is thinking about her next move
She wants to dig with her bare hands
She wants to cry, but there is no time
There is so much work to be done
Her neighbors are still entombed in their own homes

The Haitian grandmother is thinking about her grandchildren
Some of them are beneath her feet
She has to summon her courage to cry for help and rescue
Other grandkids are far away.
The Haitian grandma is like a bamboo flattened by the monsoons
She is like a coconut tree whose trunk is bent by the hurricane forces
She gets twisted by life's ups and lows,
Yet she recovers and is full of joy again
Haiti's history flashes back in her memory
The Haitian grandma survived Papa Doc, Baby Doc and the Tonton Macoutes
She survived the Zenglendo and the fast and furious gang members

Surrounded by devastation, the Haitian grandma will rise again
She will look for her family members just like a mother hen, her chicks
Scared by the nearby hawks of tumultuos weather patterns
A witness to history, she is the queen of the Haitian household
Her gaze will motivate all of us to focus on the future and rebuilding.

ISBN::
978-1-257-08365-7

www.ingramcontent.com/pod-product-compliance
Lightning Source LLC
Chambersburg PA
CBHW080446110426
42743CB00016B/3295